D0596715

How To Pray For Healing

(and what to do if nothing happens)

2nd Edition

Easy-to-follow,
step-by-step instructions
to make your prayers
for healing
more effective

Mark Dahle

A note from the author

Prayer is not a substitute for competent doctors, any more than doctors are a substitute for prayer. Ideally, both work together to promote healing. In some cases, healing doesn't come until medical treatments are done. In other cases, after the doctors have given up hope, prayer brings healing. Good doctors and good prayer partners complement each other. Both have the same goal: renewed health for you and your friends.

God bless you as you move towards the future you desire!

How To Pray For Healing (and what to do if nothing happens) 2nd Edition

© 2006, 2011 Mark Dahle

The Scripture quotations contained herein are from the *New Revised Standard Version Bible,* copyright, 1989, by the Division of Christian Education of the National Council of the Churches of Christ in the U.S.A. Used by permission. All rights reserved.

As you go, proclaim the good news,
'The kingdom of heaven has come near.'
Cure the sick,
raise the dead,
cleanse the lepers,
cast out demons.
You received without payment;
give without payment.

Matthew 10:7-8

This remarkable book details in very practical ways how you can experience healing through prayer, even if it has eluded you or your friends for years.

This book is filled with case histories and examples to help you work through the mystery of why some conditions are easily healed and why others are never resolved.

Whether you are interested in reading alone or with a group, you're about to embark on a remarkable adventure, one where you'll discover that you (and your friends) can be healed! Mark writes:

*Y*ou can be healed. Of anything. I've seen people healed of cocaine and heroin addiction. I've seen people who were healed of back pain, cancer and deformities. Even people the doctors had given up on. You can be healed, too. . . .

Acknowledgments

Several decades ago, John Wimber began reading the stories about Jesus. He read that people who followed Jesus could heal others and raise the dead, and one of his first questions was, "When do I get to do the stuff?" John wanted to get started! John's quest to learn how to heal the sick helped thousands of other people get started on the same path.

Most of the time I learned from John Wimber indirectly. John and Carol Willison taught me the basic parts of the model that I mention in chapter three. They led a small group that got me to start taking action on what I was learning. Jordan and Sonya Seng helped me see two ways Jesus prayed that I hadn't noticed before; they are included in chapter three as points two and ten. Hundreds of other friends helped by example and by sharing what they knew.

Irietys Burrows, Vicki Hesterman, Genie Hudkins, Dale Huntington, December Long, B. J. Mahla, Sue Mason, and John Townsend all read early drafts of this book and improved it with their suggestions.

This second edition includes a new chapter on healing for cases with no physical cause (Chapter 10). Thank you to everyone who offered suggestions on how to improve that chapter.

Thank you to the hundreds of other friends who also deserve to be acknowledged by name, who have tested these ideas and helped improve them. I'm grateful for your help and encouragement over the years. I especially appreciate the great people at La Jolla Lutheran Church. It is truly a privilege to be your pastor!

Contents

Sometimes healing comes easily, in an instant. Other times it requires a stubborn pursuit. The first four chapters give you some simple steps to start with. They may be all you'll need. If you need more, Section B has suggestions for people who are seeking healing for themselves but aren't healed yet. Section C has suggestions for people praying for others.

One of the best things you can do is to form a practice group to discuss this book and to pray for each other. You'll find remarkable things happen in a practice group. To help your group, each chapter ends with discussion questions to enhance your conversation. Chapter two and Appendix A give tips on setting up your group.

Section A

How To Pray For Healing

Chapter 1

You Can Be Healed

You can be healed. Of anything. I've seen people healed of cocaine and heroin addiction. I've seen people who were healed of back pain, cancer and deformities. Even people the doctors had given up on. You can be healed, too.

In seminary I was in a class that a worship leader visited to demonstrate how people in his church pray for the sick. He invited God's Spirit to be present, then waited for a minute or so. After a while, he said, "There's someone here who has a foot problem. I think we should start with that." My classmates looked at each other. There were less than 12 of us in the class. No one volunteered. John Willison, the worship leader, repeated what he'd said: "There's someone here who has a foot problem." No one moved or spoke. John waited – a long time. A third time he repeated it.

Finally, one of the class members spoke up. "Well, maybe it's me. The doctors say they may have to amputate one of my toes."

We all stared at him. Nobody thought, "No, it's probably somebody else." We all wondered, "How could you not have spoken up right away?" If John hadn't persisted, this classmate would have lost the chance for prayer simply because he didn't want to be embarrassed by admitting a need.

It's worth it to ask for help

When John prayed for this classmate, he prayed with such compassion and authority that I wanted him to pray for me, too. I didn't have any physical ailments, but I was in emotional pain. I felt like I was bleeding inside, and I knew if he prayed for me, I could be healed. But I didn't want to be embarrassed by admitting how much I needed prayer. So I quietly waited my turn in the line, not showing any outward sign how desperate I was. Although I didn't recognize the irony at the time, I was behaving just like the classmate whose reluctance to speak up had amazed me.

John prayed for each of us in order, with the same authority and compassion he used for the first classmate. When he got one person away from me he glanced at his watch. "Oh!" he exclaimed. "Look at the time! That's all for tonight!"

I couldn't believe it.

I finally found someone who might be able to heal me and he stopped one person away from praying for me. But I didn't say anything. I just stood there, feeling like I was bleeding internally, unable to admit my need.

Reaching out in faith can bring healing

In the Bible there is a story of a woman who had been bleeding for 12 years. Even though she had spent enormous amounts on doctors, she was not healed. Sanitation laws of the time demanded that she avoid contact with people until her bleeding stopped. But when Jesus came by, she defied those laws and pressed through a crowd so she could touch him. She was instantly healed.

Even though I knew that story, I hadn't let it change me. The lesson of it is clear enough: When you are in the presence of someone who is flowing with the power of God, it's worth it to reach out to that person, no matter what others might say or think, no matter how many social conventions you have to break. You don't know when the chance will come by again. But I come from a culture where the deeper the need, the less you talk about it. Once I called my mom and talked to her for half an hour. I was ready to hang up when she said, "Well, I suppose I should tell you. Your father is in the hospital. He's been there five days. We didn't want to mention it because we didn't want to worry you."

Since then my parents and I have become much better about relaying information to each other. But in the stoic culture to which I belong, you try very hard not to be a bother to anyone and you don't want to worry others. Especially if you really need help.

Maybe you can't relate to that. Some people talk incessantly about their troubles. Others are less vocal but still find it easy to admit hidden needs. But for some of us, one of the things that keeps us from getting healed is our reluctance to ask. I know people who won't mention things they're concerned about when they meet with their doctors for their annual physicals. They only get one ten-minute interview with a health professional a year, but they won't use that time to talk about what really matters.

When you miss one opportunity, create another

After John left the class, I just stood there, feeling as if I couldn't breathe. I couldn't believe how close I'd gotten to being healed – and that I had let the opportunity pass. I decided I would visit John's church.

Fortunately, at John's church dozens of people knew how to pray like John did. The first Sunday I was there, the pastor asked everyone who wanted prayer to meet with a prayer team after the service. I met three or four people who prayed for me with insight, wisdom and compassion. I wasn't healed that day, but I started to get better.

That year I joined a small group that John and his wife Carol were leading. The emphasis of the group was learning to pray for others. Part of our weekly homework assignment was to pray for someone before we got back together. As I was going home after our first session, someone near me in the subway coughed. Somehow I got up the courage to ask this stranger if I could pray for her. Since then, I've been praying for people on a fairly regular basis. Usually I'm not very bold – I don't often pray for people in subways unless I see a real need. But I have prayed for people on airplanes, in hotel lobbies, in restaurants, and in many other unlikely settings. I've seen many people healed.

Seek healing environments

At a healing service a few years ago, I was telling the story of John's visit to our class. I emphasized how helpful it was for people to admit their needs – and how hard it is for some of us. I encouraged people to admit their needs and receive the healing they desired. I really pressed the point of asking for help. Many people responded, and we prayed for them. Dale was one who did not respond.

Dale had been a spectator at a football game the day before, even though his back was causing tremendous pain. He hurt so much he couldn't reach for the drink in the cup holder next to his chair. He had to have his daughter lift the drink to his lips. At our healing service, he was still in pain. He sat through the story of the man facing amputation who wouldn't admit his need. He sat through the story of my own inability to ask for help. He sat through my best efforts to encourage everyone who needed prayer to seize the opportunity. But he didn't respond.

In spite of that, God healed him. No one touched him and no one prayed for him directly. But he walked out of the service freed of the pain. "I felt like dancing," he told me later.

Sometimes healing is like that. It's just in the air and it catches us, almost by surprise. Other times healing evades us, no matter how hard we try to pursue it.

Learn from people who excel

If you want to do something, experts suggest that you find a person who is really good at what you want to do and copy that person's approach. This advice applies whether you want to be good at sales, sports, business or some other field.

If you wanted to copy the approach of someone good at healing, who would you choose? Who has the greatest success rate?

We could name many people alive today. But in terms of human history, probably the person with the most success was Jesus. Jesus healed people of all the difficult illnesses of his day, including epilepsy, deafness, blindness, incurable bleeding, leprosy, paralysis, and even demon possession. Jesus taught his followers to pray for people and to heal them, announcing, "The kingdom of heaven has come near you."

Two thousand years later, followers of Jesus are still healing people through the power of prayer.

People report being healed of alcoholism, drug addiction, cancer, mobility problems and a wide variety of physical diseases, as well as mental, emotional and spiritual distress.

Given Jesus' credentials as a healer and a teacher, you might think that many people would follow his methods. Amazingly, many people either have forgotten, have not adopted, or have never noticed the way Jesus taught his followers to pray for healing. As a result, many of us can learn a lot by modeling our prayers after his. In chapter three, we'll look at what Jesus taught about praying for healing.

Chapter two discusses how to get the most out of this book.

Questions for Discussion

1) What have you been healed from in the past?

2) What helped your healing?

3) What conditions do you have that aren't healed yet?

4) How easy is it for you to admit your needs to friends?

5) Prayer is talking to God who loves you. How easy is it for you to talk over your needs with God?

6) What in this chapter caught your attention?

Chapter 2

One Great Way To Begin

One of the best things you can do when learning how to pray for healing is to invite five or six friends to practice with you. Your group can read a chapter in this book, talk about it, then take turns praying for each other. When you practice in a group, it will be easier to quickly make progress, because you will learn from everyone else's experiences.

Using the techniques outlined in this book, I've seen people freed from cancer, back trouble, joint problems, drug addiction, and many other conditions. In your group, you'll likely see many wonderful things happen as well.

One powerful secret will increase your success rate

Early in his career, a financial planner met a couple who had done what few people accomplish: They had set aside enough money from a modest income to retire early and live well. The planner probed for their secret. He was earning more than them, but he was finding it difficult to save for *his* retirement. He knew all the theory, but it wasn't enough to help him take the right action. So what did *they* do?

The couple taught him a secret that has broad application, far beyond financial planning. Practicing this secret will help you achieve goals that have eluded you thus far, whether your goals are related to finances, fitness, relationships or something else (like healing!).

The couple knew they wanted to save for retirement, but they also knew they would be tempted to spend their money instead of saving it. How could they make sure they always did what was right for their long-term future?

The secret they discovered was to never face a choice about it. They made the right action happen automatically. In their case, they had money deducted from their pay before they got their checks. They never were tempted to do anything with the money because they never had access to it. They made the decision to save once – automated it – and never faced it again.[1]

Following their strategy and making things happen automatically can help you in areas where you know the right thing to do but don't always do it. Set up a process where you never face the choice. Make it so the right thing happens automatically, no matter what you do. (We'll discuss how this advice applies to healing prayer after a brief observation.)

Make getting help automatic

One thing have I noticed over years of praying for healing is that many of us can have an acute need, be in the presence of a solution, and *still* not ask for help.

In the next chapter, you will learn a very effective model to use when praying for healing. Then, in the chapters that follow, you will learn strategies for cases where the initial prayer doesn't produce immediate results. But the amazing truth is:

* Some people who desperately need healing will have the book but not read it. Things will get in the way, including their own ambivalence about getting well. (Maybe they feel they don't deserve health, maybe it'll take too much effort, maybe something else will be more pressing.)

* Some will read the book but will not take action. They'll have all the knowledge they need to be healed, but they won't take the simple steps required to be free.

* Some will start taking action but let other things get in the way before they see results.

* Some will experience wonderful, dramatic healing of one condition and be grateful – and then set the ideas aside and go no further.

* Only a few will read, start to practice, experience results, and then *keep on going*, healing people around them and receiving healing themselves on a regular basis.

So how can we get into that last group, where ongoing renewal becomes a part of who we are? We know we *want* to be there, but we don't always follow through with what is best.

The secret is to automate what we want to do. Arrange to have it happen automatically.

Set up a practice group

An easy way to automate getting prayer for healing on a regular basis is to invite a group of friends to practice praying with you. When you get together, you can read a chapter of this book, discuss it, and then pray for each other, using the model in chapter three. This way, every time you meet you'll get prayer for one of your own needs and you'll automatically get practice praying for others. As you compare notes with friends week after week, you'll learn much faster than you would on your own.

Ask yourself: Who do you want in your group?

What are their phone numbers?

Call the people on your list and invite them now, before you change your mind about taking action! Then check Appendix A for tips that will help your group become successful.

Is your group formed?

I see you're still reading. Did you call anyone yet?

Yes – I formed my group.

> Congratulations! You've taken a step that can lead to one of the best adventures of your life!

Yes – but I got discouraged before I got enough people for my group.

> Groups can be any size, but to speed your learning, it is often helpful to have several participants. At this stage you might tell God you're discouraged and ask for ideas of people to invite. If you're not used to talking to God, it's like talking to your best friend. You can tell God anything. In this case, you could ask for the excitement and energy to encourage people to join your group. If you need a break, schedule a specific time tomorrow when you'll make more calls. But don't lose out on this opportunity. Your group is a great adventure waiting to happen, and it's worth pursuing through obstacles. What time will you make more calls tomorrow?

No, I didn't call anyone yet.

> Make a list of people you'd like in your group and start calling! Or, if that's too hard, ask an organized friend to help you form the group. Who do you know (that you would like to be in the group) who is organized enough to call others and make it happen? Ask this person to organize the group.

Some people will be healed just by reading this book. But even more will be healed when they meet in small groups and pray with friends. If you take action on this, you'll find you and your friends will be healed of more conditions than if you don't. It's worth it for your sake and for theirs to get a group together.

Checklist

_____ Identify people you would like to be part of your group.

_____ Invite them to an introductory session.

_____ When you get together, review the list at the start of chapter three. Have each person identify something he or she wants prayer for. Take turns praying for each person in the group.

_____ Invite the people back find out what happened and to learn more about prayer.

_____ Read Appendix A for more hints on forming your group.

_____ By the second session, have your group review the suggestions in Appendix A and agree which ones your group will keep.

Questions for Discussion

1) What are some good things to do that you sometimes leave undone?

2) Which of these would you like to happen automatically?

3) What would be an effective way to get them to happen automatically?

4) When will you set that up?

5) What else in this chapter caught your attention?

Chapter 3

One Model For Prayer

Some of the people I've trained to pray for healing were complete beginners. They had never prayed aloud before, let alone prayed for someone for healing. They were quickly amazed to see that God used them and their prayers in spite of their lack of experience. If you're in this group, you'll be amazed, too.

Other people I've trained have had quite a bit of practice. If you're in this second group, you may have a favorite way to pray. Many people do. If so, I encourage you to keep at it. But I also I encourage you to experiment with the model outlined in this chapter.

The steps of this model are based on how Jesus prayed for people. I'm not suggesting you give up the other ways you pray. But test this approach and compare its results with the results you get with other styles of prayer. I think you'll find if you try this model – even though many aspects of it may seem unfamiliar at first – you will be happy with the results. And if you've never prayed before, this will be a great way for you to begin talking to God who loves you. You'll find talking to God is as natural as talking to your best friend.

First I'll list the steps of the model, then I'll go over them one at a time to explain them.

Pray like Jesus

1) Pray every chance you get.

2) When you're ready to pray for someone, move away from people who are openly scoffing or get them to leave the area where you are.

3) Ask the people you're praying for what they want.

4) Ask for permission to place your hands on people's heads or shoulders while you pray.

5) Tell people you're going to be quiet for a minute before you pray for them. Out loud, pray, "God, help us become more aware of your presence." Then pause for a time of quiet.

6) Silently ask, "God, what would *you* like me to pray about?" Pause and listen.

7) Pray about things you sense in your body, in your mind, in your spirit, and in your heart.

8) Keep your eyes open. You may see something important!

9) If you have doubts while you are praying, don't express them. Instead, pray what the Bible teaches.

10) Speak directly to the condition and tell it what to do.

11) After praying, ask people what they are experiencing.

12) Pray until the energy seems to be gone or until the person stops receiving.

Here's a brief explanation of each of the points:

Pray at every opportunity

1) Pray every chance you get._

Prayer is talking to God who loves you. It's something Jesus did all the time. He was known for getting away by himself to pray. He also prayed in crowds. He frequently prayed for people who were sick.[1]

It's helpful for us to adopt this habit of frequently talking to God. And it's also helpful to adopt Jesus' habit of praying for the sick on a regular basis. As we practice, we become more effective. With practice, we begin to see patterns; we learn what actions are helpful in particular circumstances; we learn ways that God gives us insight into what to do next.

Paul was a follower of Jesus who wrote many letters that are included in the Bible. In one of the letters he wrote:

> Rejoice always, <u>pray without ceasing</u>, give thanks in all circumstances; for this is the will of God in Christ Jesus for you.[2]

Fortunately, it's easy to pray without ceasing since so many people need help. If we keep our eyes and ears open, we will never run out of opportunities to pray for people.

Pray with people of faith

2) When you're ready to pray for someone, either move away from people who are scoffing or get them to leave the area where you are.

The Bible reports that Jesus "did not do many deeds of power [in his hometown] because of their unbelief."[3] In other cities, Jesus had done miraculous things. But the people in his hometown had such low expectations that he wasn't able to do much for them. *His* ability was hindered by *their* disbelief. If Jesus himself was stopped by the disbelief of people around him, we should probably move away from disbelieving people when we pray for others.

When Jesus brought a twelve-year-old girl back to life, he cleared the room of scoffers and allowed only his closest friends and the family members to stay.[4] You'll probably also have better results if you move away from doubters or ask them to leave. Fortunately, it's very easy to move to a space where you can be alone with people who have hope.

When I'm doing this, I watch for people who actively

discourage others in the room, either by their words, facial expressions, body position or presence. These are the people I want to move away from. I'm happy to include people with doubts in their minds but hope in their hearts. Jesus helped a father like this.[5] Many days I'm like that, too! For those of us who experience both doubt and faith, one thing that helps is to intentionally call to mind all the times Jesus has healed in the past. Remembering these events can give hope for what Jesus will do today.

Ask people what they want

3) Ask people you're praying for what they want.

It's not always as obvious as you think! One lame man that Jesus healed needed forgiveness as much as he needed the ability to walk. (He got both.)[6] Sometimes people in wheelchairs will want prayer for their finances or a relative rather than their own physical conditions. Let people tell you what they want.

Jesus modeled this several times, once with a blind man begging outside Jericho. When the man cried out, "Have mercy on me!" Jesus asked him, "What do you want me to do for you?" Some might assume the answer was obvious. The man begged from everyone; perhaps he wanted money. But Jesus' question allowed him to state his highest wish: "Lord, let me see again."[7]

When you ask people what they want, some will give just the right amount of information. Suppose Gary says, "I was in a car accident five years ago and I've had leg pain ever since. Sometimes it hurts so bad I can't sleep." That's just right. Knowing the cause and the approximate time something occurred is not necessary, but it is helpful. If Gary's accident occurred only a week ago, his body still might reset itself on its own. Since his accident was five years ago, you know his pain is not going to go away without some kind of change. Knowing the cause (in this case, a car accident) also lets you ask about and pray for any mental or emotional trauma. Knowing the present symptoms (pain and disruption of sleep) lets you pray directly into the most obvious area of hurt. You can pray for healing of both the symptoms and their cause.

When you ask people what they want prayer for, some will give you little or no information. Sometimes this is because they don't know what they want. Other times they know quite clearly, but their stories can't be told. And other times they know what they want but are not self-confident enough to voice such hopes. In all these cases, trust that God knows the situation. Pray with confidence, asking God to address their deepest needs.

When you ask people what they want, a few will try to tell you far more than you need to know. You're not trying to provide counseling, you're offering to bring them to an awareness of God who loves them. So if the situation is too complicated to be easily described, have them summarize it in five words or less. If you don't interrupt some people, they will focus on their misfortunes and troubles instead of on God's ability to set them free. If a person has just given a long, graphic description of troubles, it might be helpful to remind the person of all the people God has already healed. This will help get the focus off the person's troubles and onto the One who can heal.

Ask for permission to place your hands on people's heads or shoulders

4) Ask for permission to place your hands on people's heads or shoulders while you pray.

If they say no, it's fine. But God's Spirit is often transmitted by touch,[8] and Jesus and his disciples often placed their hands on people when healing them.[9] Even if nothing else happens, many times people experience mercy when you gently touch them, because they know you care.

In some cases it may be appropriate to ask permission to place your hand on the place where people are experiencing pain. If an ear needs healing, or an ankle, in many cultures touching these areas is acceptable. Other areas of the body are more sensitive and should not be touched. Because many painful experiences are often hidden, err on the side of caution. You can place your hands in the air about six inches from the spot you are praying for or place your hand on the person's head if the person agrees to it. And if the person doesn't want you this close, God can still move with power. Jesus healed people who were far from his presence with just a word.[10] You can, too.

Focus on God before you begin

5) Tell people you're going to be quiet for a minute before you pray for them.

Out loud, pray, "God, help us become more aware of your presence." Then pause for a time of quiet. This helps everyone remember that it is God who heals. And in the silence, you may feel God prompting you for what the first step should be.

One time a woman was accused of a crime that had the death penalty. The religious leaders pressed Jesus for his thoughts on the matter. Rather than responding immediately, Jesus began writing in the dirt, essentially taking a time out. When he finally answered their questions, he had an answer that was worth waiting for.[11] When we pause to listen to God, we often receive very helpful insights for what to do next.

6) Silently ask, "God, what would you *like me to pray about?" Pause and listen.*

One of the secrets of Jesus' success is that he only did what he saw God doing.[12] When we follow God's direction, we will be able to accomplish far more than if we just start off on our own.

Once I was praying for a woman who told me the condition she wanted prayer for – I think it was her arm. While she was describing her symptoms, I felt a terrific pain in my ear. As you practice praying for people, you'll begin to pick up clues like this. So when she was done talking, I said I'd be happy to pray for her arm, but first I was going to pray for her left ear. She became very excited because the ear I mentioned had been punctured recently. Because I was able to pick up that unspoken need, she was much more receptive to receiving prayer about her original request.

Be open to intuitions from God

7) *Pray about things you sense in your body, in your mind, in your spirit, and in your heart. Filter your impressions through your knowledge of God and God's ways.*

Many people are not used to praying out loud. Like any activity, it becomes more comfortable as you get some practice. It helps to pray out loud so people you're praying for can relax and agree with your prayers.

When you pray, if you stay sensitive to impressions in your mind and body, you will discover quite a mix of information. You may have thoughts of doubt and faith at the same time. You may sense pain or heat or pressure or tingling in particular parts of your body. You may have impressions or intuitions. Some of these will be from God. Some will not. How can you tell which is which?

There's good news and bad news here. The good news is that as you practice, you'll become better at recognizing which impressions are likely to be accurate. The bad news is that there is never certainty about which impressions are from God – you'll always be learning and relying on God's mercy. I think part of the reason for this is that God wants to have an ongoing relationship with us, and our being uncertain inspires us to stay in conversation with God.

As you practice, however, I have found some general guidelines to be useful.

Some intuitions should be discarded

If you're sensing something that contradicts what you know about God, discard it or pray against it, silently or out loud.

Let's say you have the thought that you should quit because you're looking like a fool. Is that thought from God or not? Maybe you know from reading about the prophets of God that many of them looked foolish at God's command. God doesn't seem to mind it when people look like fools.[13] Based on this knowledge, you know you can discard the thought of quitting. Something good is going on – and your own pride or embarrassment or sense of shame is kicking up. Stay with it.

Suppose while praying for someone you had the thought "This person is not worth it." You know that's *not* what God would think. God loves each of us far more than we can imagine.

You could simply discard the thought. But sometimes when we have thoughts like this we are picking up something that the person we're praying for feels. You can experiment by asking the person about it or by praying something you know to be true that opposes the idea. In the case of the thought, "This person is not worth it," I might pray some ideas expressed in the Bible, "God, thank you that this person is highly esteemed in your eyes. Thank you that he is worth your favor. Thank you that you counted him worthy even when he was rejecting your ways.[14] Thank you that you have loved him from the moment of his conception.[15] Thank you that he is perfectly and wonderfully made.[16] Thank you that you will always be with him, loving him, no matter where he goes."[17]

Since I have my eyes open, I will be able to see his reaction. Sometimes a tear will form as he accepts the truth of God's unconditional love. On the other hand, if he flinches or if it looks like he can't accept what I just said, I might talk to him about it. If he replied that he felt rejected, I might pray that he would experience God's amazing acceptance. You could also tell the feeling of rejection to leave and invite God's Spirit to fill the place the rejection had occupied.

This business of dealing with intuitions is inexact – show yourself some mercy. But if you maintain a loving attitude toward your own choices and the people you are praying for, they will know and experience your acceptance, even if you don't guess right about the intuitions you have.

If you have an impression, ask about it

If you sense pain in a part of your body, or tingling, or light, or cold or heat – any sensation that is not accounted for by the room temperature or other natural events – ask the people you are praying for if something is going on in that area. Like a baseball batter, you'll probably swing and miss sometimes. That's how you learn. Over time you'll learn which sensations are most likely to be accurate clues and which are not.

(If the tingling is in your hands, it may be an indication that energy is in you, waiting to be released when you place your hands on the other person. If your hands are already touching the person, silently ask God to remove any resistance and let God's power flow into the other person. Ask this silently so the other person's focus can stay on God.)

It's also good to ask people you're praying for about intuitions you have – pictures you sense in your imagination and other impressions. If what you sense is not pertinent, people will know. In my own experience, if I have a thought that I "hear" as if someone were speaking, it's often wrong or random, so I rarely voice these. This is especially true if the thought comes as a command. But if I have a very faint impression about something, it's usually true. As you experiment over time, you'll find out what kinds of things are usually accurate for you.

Follow intuitions that seem to be from God

Once I was going to preach at a church in my hometown,

a small city in Alaska. The service was broadcast on the radio station that everyone listened to. As I prepared my message, I had the clear sense that I needed to mention that adultery was not part of God's plan.

I didn't want to say this. My overall message was about something else, and I knew that friends of mine who avoided church would be listening to the broadcast. One of my friends loved to find weekend partners on a regular basis. I didn't want her to think that I didn't accept her.

Some people would have been *eager* to use the radio to confront my friend! But that's not my style. Anyway, as the day approached I couldn't shake the feeling. So at some point in the message, I said something about how adultery is not what God intends and that people involved in it would be happier if they changed their ways. I did not dwell on it, but I said it.

The next day, my fears were confirmed. My friend had listened to the broadcast, and she wanted to know what I meant – not about the main message I had delivered, but about that one short part about adultery. I told her I didn't judge her, but at the same time, her actions weren't healthy for herself or others.

Soon afterwards, she began following Jesus. She joined a church, became a committed Christian, married a man and continued her lively interest in sex within the healthy boundary of marriage. Her life was transformed in many wonderful ways.

Something else also happened. About three weeks after my message, two people who had heard it left town. They had been having a secret affair for some time. When they left, they broke apart two families. The families were devastated and the church was shocked. I was very unhappy with their decision, but I was also glad I had been obedient. I think my message was one of God's last attempts to get through to this couple that what they were doing was wrong and they could still turn from it. As it turned out, they chose against God's purposes for their lives. But they had an opportunity for repentance before their devastating secret became public.

Following intuitions is worth it, even if you don't see results

If you have an intuition, you may feel awkward mentioning it, as I did. But as you experiment, you will probably discover that many of your intuitions are worth voicing. People will be able to forgive you if you are wrong, especially if you ask in a spirit of gentleness and humility.

Let's say that you're talking to someone and, while you are talking, you sense embezzlement is a factor. Ask.

If it is not, in most cases the person will say no and you can move on. Sometimes the person will say no but ask why you brought it up. If so, just tell them that you were curious. "If embezzlement doesn't mean anything to you, don't dwell on it. It just came to me, so I thought I'd ask."

One of three things will occur at this point. First, if you *did* make a mistake, you made it in a way that was gracious enough that most people will be able to forgive you and move on. It's part of the learning curve. Second, if you were right but they don't realize it yet, God will make it plain to them in due time. And third, if you were right but they weren't willing to admit it, you've given them the information they need: God loves them and their sin is not hidden. Knowing that, they will be able to make a choice about whether they want to follow God or their sin. You've laid the groundwork. You may hear the end of the story later or you may not. In the meantime, move on to the next thing that seems worth praying about.

While you are praying, watch for visual cues

8) Keep your eyes open. You may see something important!

This piece of advice will be very difficult for some, because many of us have grown used to praying with our hands folded and eyes closed. It's fine to pray like that all you want at other times. But when you pray for healing, if you keep your eyes open you will be much more effective.

Once when I was praying for a woman I said something about how much God loved her. She silently shook her head "No." I kept on praying, and said again that God really loved her. Again she silently shook her head, "No." If I'd had my eyes closed, I would have missed it. Since I was watching, I saw her unintentionally reveal her inner thoughts. Before praying further, I was able to ask her directly if she thought God loved her – and we were able to work through her deep-seated doubt that *anyone* could love her. Talking this through made the rest of the prayer much more effective.

If you keep your eyes open, you'll see many things like that. What you observe may help you refocus your prayers or ask helpful questions. You may see a tear forming in someone's eye. You may see someone flinch. You may see someone's face take on a recognizable emotion, indicating how that person is responding. You may see someone's eyelids flutter, indicating that the person's visual imagination is engaged. Over time, you'll learn to recognize many of the ways that people respond unconsciously to prayer and you'll grow in effectiveness.

If you're used to keeping your eyes closed, keeping them open may feel uncomfortable at first, and it may require some self-discipline, but it will be worth it if you persist.

Pray what the Bible teaches, not your doubts

9) If you have doubts while you are praying, don't express them. Instead, pray what the Bible teaches.

People praying their doubts might say,

"God, we don't know what's going on for Linda."

Instead of this, they could pray what the Bible says:

"God, you know exactly what's going on for Linda."

The first prayer gets the focus onto themselves and their inadequacy. The second prayer puts the focus where it belongs, on God and God's ability.

Similarly, I'd encourage you to pray about the positive future you desire instead of the present distress. For example someone talking about the present distress might pray,

"God, Linda is lonely. She thinks no one cares. She feels abandoned."

I've heard people pray in this way so descriptively and for such a long time that if Linda didn't start out depressed, she had a good chance of being so by the middle of the prayer. The person unintentionally gave Linda vivid word pictures of why she should give up hope.

Most of the time, I think it is better to pray about the positive reality and the hoped-for future.

"God, thank you that you have always been with Linda. Thank you that you have always cared for her. Thank you that you have been with her throughout her life. Help her to experience more of your love. Thank you that you are helping her find great friends she can trust. Thank you that she can trust you with her future."

If Linda's core hurt was loneliness, this prayer could be expanded with vivid word pictures that could fill Linda with hope about the kind of friends God will help her find in the coming weeks.

The Bible contains many wonderful promises. Some probably relate to the situation of people you're praying for. If you know some of those promises, you can include them in your prayers.

For instance, you could ask for Jim, a man with heart arrhythmia:

> Jesus, when you went throughout Galilee, you healed every disease.[18] There was nothing too great for you, no condition too difficult. Thank you that you are the same yesterday and today and forever.[19] Thank you that you have the power to heal Jim today. In your name, Jesus, we tell Jim's heart to stabilize and to return to normal functioning. Thank you. Amen.

Speak directly to the condition

10) Speak directly to the condition and tell it what to do.

Many people don't have a lot of confidence when they pray for people, and their prayers for healing reflect it. Their words have little power. They say things like:

> "God, I'm sorry Robert is so sick. Please be with him."

There's nothing wrong with God being with Robert when Robert is sick, but to ask for that misunderstands a lot about God. God is with everyone before anyone asks. So at a minimum, ask, "God, help Robert become fully aware of your presence with him." If Robert became fully aware of God's presence and love for him, he would be healed in spirit, if not in body. But at this point, what Robert most wants is probably to get better or to be out of pain. Ask him what he wants and pray about that. Unfortunately, sometimes people praying don't have any confidence that Robert will get better and "don't want to get Robert's hopes up."

Sometimes people's words don't give away their lack of hope, but you can tell from their tone of voice that they don't think prayer will help.

Other times people have more confidence and they pray more boldly:

"God, we believe you will heal Robert of cancer. Thank you."

This is a fine approach, especially when it is done humbly. When Jesus healed people, however, he did not follow this method. Instead, he healed through words of command:

* Jesus told a man with leprosy, "Be made clean."[20]

* He told a paralyzed man, "Stand up, take your bed, and go to your home." [21]

* He put his fingers in a deaf man's ears and said "Be opened." [22]

* He commanded spirits that were tormenting people, "Come out." [23]

* He told a blind man, "Receive your sight." [24]

* He told a woman bent over, "You are set free from your ailment." [25]

* He told a widow's dead son, "Young man, I say to you, rise." [26]

* He told a man with a withered hand, "Stretch out your hand."[27]

* He told a dead girl, "Little girl, get up." [28]

* He told a dead friend, "Lazarus, come out (of your tomb)." [29]

* He even calmed a storm by telling it, "Be still." [30]

Notice that in all these cases, Jesus addressed the person or the situation directly and commanded either health to appear or the illness to leave.

Some might assume that commanding afflictions was something only Jesus could do. But the records we have of the healing done by the early disciples of Jesus show that Jesus taught them to follow his approach:

> * Peter told a lame man, "In the name of Jesus Christ of Nazareth, stand up and walk."[31]

> * Peter told a paralyzed man, "Jesus Christ heals you; get up and make your bed!" [32]

> * He told a dead girl, "Get up." [33]

> * Similarly, Paul, who never met Jesus except in a vision, said to a crippled man, "Stand upright on your feet." [34]

> * Paul told a demon afflicting a girl, "I order you in the name of Jesus Christ to come out of her." [35]

Be simple and direct

Many people try to heal through intercession. ("God, please help Bob recover.") What would happen if instead we copied the example of Jesus and his early followers and healed through words of command? ("Bob, in Jesus name, become well.")

Intercession has its place – often before speaking the word of command it helps our faith if we silently ask God for wisdom, faith, boldness or whatever we need. (We do this silently so we don't discourage people receiving prayer by getting them to focus our lack of confidence instead of God's ability.) But when you are ready to heal someone by the power of God, consider using words that are straightforward and simple. "Recover." "Cancer, disappear." "AIDS, leave." "Blood vessels, return to normal." "Back, align yourself correctly."

One of the first objections people have to speaking like this is that they feel they have no power to speak so boldly. That's true, and it's good to acknowledge it. Your power to heal people does not come from you, it comes from God. In order to command a back to be aligned correctly, we have to align <u>ourselves</u> correctly under God's command. As we do so, we speak not on our own authority but on the authority of God who loves us.

Jesus told his followers to teach people to observe everything he commanded.[36] He taught the motivation for this great project had to be love.[37] He also taught the *way* his disciples were to fulfill this command – when he sent out his followers, he told them to do five things:

* announce good news to the poor

* heal the sick

* raise the dead

* cleanse the lepers

* cast out demons[38]

Clearly, we need more practice on most of these. But as we pray for the sick to be healed, we're following the direct command of Jesus. Our authority comes from him. Since that's the case, let's follow the model of Jesus and his early disciples and speak to the conditions directly. If you're like me, this may take some practice for you to get used to it. But it's usually better to follow a model that works than our own opinions.

Ask people if anything happened

11) After praying, ask people what they are experiencing.

Jesus modeled this when healing a blind man. When he asked if the man could see, he discovered the man was only partially healed, leading to a second prayer. After the second prayer, the man's sight was fully restored.[39] If you pray and the condition is better but not fully healed, pray some more. (Sometimes the healing will continue over the course of the next day or week. But it's worth it to pray a second time if your results are incomplete. Often a second prayer will bring greater results.)

Sometimes people feel a sensation of heat, cold, light, heaviness, calm, peace or the like. It is usually worth it to spend a few more minutes in prayer, blessing what God is doing in such cases. Don't be disappointed if the person reports no sensations, however. People often are totally healed without any immediate sensation or knowledge that healing has taken place.

12) Pray until the energy seems to be gone or until the recipient stops receiving.

If people you are praying for break off the connection, you can gently encourage them to stay open to what God is doing if you think there is more for them. Talking them through the process is often helpful. But if they still want to quit, let them quit. You can intercede for them after they have gone if you think there is more to be done.

Most of the time, I am the one who is tempted to quit early, even though I can feel energy for more prayer. Perhaps you will experience the desire to quit early as well.

Imagine what you'd think of a doctor who became unhappy a surgery was taking so long and left in the middle of it. Surely you don't want to be like *that*! Prayer for people's deep hurts is just as important to complete as surgery – and sometimes it can have effects far more profound when we follow it through to completion. You may have to overcome embarrassment or shame or other emotions to continue, but the results are worth it.

Have confidence even if nothing seems to happen

13) Don't expect fireworks all the time.

This isn't on the list at the start of the chapter, but I add it here. Many times you may not feel especially inspired when you are praying. That won't affect your results. There have been times when I have thought, "That didn't go anywhere." But the people were healed. You just never know. You're not trying for fireworks. You're trying to bring the presence and love of God to people. That can happen even when you don't sense anything in the moment.

Finally, five social conventions that will probably be helpful:

* If someone wants privacy, move to a visible corner of an open room where others are present. Don't pray for someone behind closed doors, especially if it's only going to be you and the person getting prayer. If you can, include a number of people on the prayer team.

* One exception might be if a person becomes highly agitated while you are praying and it is disturbing others. If you move to a nearby room, bring a group with you to help you pray.

* Many prayer teams have men pray for men and women pray for women. This is often helpful.

* Some churches ask their prayer teams to take breath mints before praying for others. It's a good habit.

* Follow the "house rules" of the facility where you are. The leaders may ask you to not pray or to pray with a member of their team. They may ask you to pray a particular way. Accept their rules or don't participate. When you're in your own facility, you can set the rules you like.

Practice steps that feel uncomfortable – you'll improve

Some of the steps outlined in this chapter may seem very natural to you; others may feel awkward at first or even wrong.

It's worth it to suspend judgment for a month or two while you get some practice. At the end of that time you can decide if you like the results compared to the results you were getting before.

Ultimately, of course, the best approach is not any *particular* way that one applies like a cookie cutter to all situations but rather the way that God's Spirit is leading you in the moment. But it's often helpful to have a starting spot, and I think you'll find this model is a good place to begin. If you're afraid of stepping out, that's normal. As you take action, you will gain experience and discover the benefits of praying this way.

The best thing you can do at this point is to get some practice. Charles Finney once said,

> It is not my design to preach so as to have you able to say at the close: 'We understand all about [it] now,' while you do nothing. I want you as fast as you learn anything on the subject . . . to put it in practice.[40]

Find someone who is sick or has a long-term condition. That'll be about half the people you know. Maybe more. Ask some of them if you can pray for them. Take this book and keep it open to the checklist on the next page. Go down the list, one point at a time. Explain to the people that you're learning a new method but that God is powerful even though you are a beginner. That'll take some pressure off you and them. It won't be long before the whole process becomes natural, and you won't need to check the list in this book. Or better yet, invite a group over to your house so you can all learn together.

Some people will be completely healed the first time you pray for them. Others will start to recover with one prayer. Others won't have their conditions change, but they'll know you care. After you've gotten some practice, review chapter nine for tips on how to increase your effectiveness. Meanwhile, you can use the summary on the next page for easy reference when you pray.

Checklist

_____ Pray every chance you get.

_____ Keep a tin of breath mints handy.

_____ When you're ready to pray for someone, either move away from people who are openly scoffing or get them to leave the area where you are.

_____ Ask the people you're praying for what they want.

_____ Ask for permission to place your hands on people's heads or shoulders while you pray.

_____ Tell people you're going to be quiet in God's presence before you pray for them. Out loud, pray, "God, help us become more aware of your presence." Then pause for a time of quiet.

_____ Silently ask, "God, what would *you* like me to pray about?" Pause and listen.

_____ Pray about things you sense in your body, in your mind, in your spirit, and in your heart.

_____ Keep your eyes open. You may see something important!

_____ If you have doubts while you are praying, don't express them. Pray what the Bible teaches, not your doubts.

_____ Speak directly to the condition and tell it what to do.

_____ After praying, ask people what they are experiencing.

_____ Pray until the energy seems to be gone or until the person stops receiving.

Questions for Discussion

1) What concepts were new to you?

2) What steps do you need to practice the most?

3) What would you like prayer for today?

4) If you're not in a group, who will you meet with to pray about the above condition? When will you meet?

5) After you've had a chance to pray with someone, talk about your experience. What did you notice?

6) What did you wonder about?

7) What surprised you?

8) What delighted you?

9) What else in this chapter caught your attention?

Chapter 4

What To Do If You're Already Healed

Some people will have been healed already, just by reading this far, even without prayer. Others will have assembled their group, gotten prayer and been healed. This chapter gives six suggestions for people who have been healed:

Thank God

1) Praise and thank God.

It's good to praise and thank God at all times, including when you are healed. A songwriter says in Psalm 103:

> Bless the LORD, O my soul,
> and all that is within me, bless his holy name.
> Bless the LORD, O my soul,
> and do not forget all his benefits–
> who forgives all your iniquity,
> who heals all your diseases.[1]

In one of the stories of Jesus healing people, only one person in ten returned to give thanks. But that one was commended for his actions.[2] Being thankful puts us in a posture where we can experience peace, love and joy and more of God's blessing. It's good to be in the group that gives thanks.

Be a blessing to others

2) Help others.

A second thing you can do when you're healed is to help others. Hopefully you were blessing others even *before* you were healed. If everyone waited to be completely well before helping others, few people would be helped! In fact, one of the things that often *brings* healing is to help others. Many times when people take their minds off their own conditions and help others, they find their troubles disappear – sometimes in the moment, sometimes forever. But even though you can give a lot of help to others when you are hurting, you can often give even more when you are healed. Paul, an early follower of Jesus, wrote that God consoles us when we are distressed so we can later console others.[3] People who are healed will find even greater joy when they begin blessing others with the mercy they have received.

This point of being a blessing is far more important than you might think at first. Hezekiah was a king of Israel who became very ill. God told Isaiah to tell him to put his affairs in order because he was going to die. When Hezekiah heard the news, he turned to the wall and wept, praying, "Remember now, O Lord, I implore you, how I have walked before you in faithfulness with a whole heart, and have done what is good in your sight."[4] The prayer so moved God that before Isaiah got out of the palace, God told him to go back and announce that Hezekiah would be healed in three days and live another 15 years.

Unfortunately, this story doesn't have a happy ending. During those 15 years, Hezekiah fathered a son who became one of the most wicked kings ever seen in Israel. Many people later regretted that Hezekiah recovered.

Hezekiah's story shows us that recovering from illness is only the first step. Far more important is what you do once you have recovered. You can be a blessing. Or you can make choices that cause people generations later to regret that you lived so long. Don't do *that!*

Share your story

3) Share your story.

In addition to thanking God and being a blessing to others, you can share your story with people who are hurting. People who are hurting need to know that there is hope – and where they can find help. Sharing your story will encourage others to keep on the path towards healing.

Be sensible

4) Be sensible.

I was at a conference where a pastor's back was healed. It had been hurting him for a long time. He received prayer and the pain disappeared for the first time in years. The next evening he returned, asking for more prayer. He had felt so good he decided to haul some cement bags around, and now he was hurting again.

You can have more sense than this friend. Don't carry bags of cement the day after your back is healed.

Shake off returning symptoms

5) Shake off returning symptoms.

Even if you are sensible, however, you may experience what feels like an old symptom returning at some point. Many people find they can shake it off and return to a state of total health by acting as if the symptom isn't there. Instead of focusing on temporary setbacks, keep focused on your new-found health.

Spend more time with Jesus

6) Learn more from Jesus.

Finally, you can read more of the stories about Jesus to see if you can gain anything else from his teaching. A blind man was one of the few people Jesus met who did this. Many people came to Jesus with a particular condition; when that was cured, they walked away, happy. But the blind man did something extraordinary. After he gained his sight, he followed Jesus, praising God.[5] Because he expressed his gratitude and stayed near the one who could heal others, he had a chance to hear some of Jesus' amazing teaching.

Who knows what other benefits he gained, simply because he stayed around longer than others who were healed. You can follow this man's good example.

To recap: When you are healed, give thanks to God, be a blessing to others, share your story, be sensible, walk in your new freedom as you grow in health, and spend some time listening to Jesus to see if he can teach you anything else.

Chapters five through eight have strategies for people who aren't healed yet. Chapters nine and ten have strategies for people praying *for others* who aren't healed yet.

Checklist

_____ When you've been healed, thank God. Repeatedly.

_____ Be a blessing to others.

_____ Tell others what happened. Encourage people that God can heal them, too.

_____ Be sensible the first week and don't overdo it.

_____ Shake off any symptoms that come back.

_____ Read about Jesus to see if he can help you with anything else.

Questions for Discussion

1) What do you have to be thankful for?

2) What are ways you have been a blessing to others in the past?

3) What would you like to do in the future to bless others?

4) Who would benefit from hearing part of your story?

5) Are you inclined to carry bags of cement the day after you are healed? Or to take it easy, long after you could be working? Or something in between those two?

6) What else in this chapter caught your attention?

Section B

Ideas For People
Who Are Not Healed Yet

Chapter 5

What To Do If You're Not Healed Yet

Sometimes people ask God for healing and they are healed immediately. I met Percy when he was in his 70s. I don't think a day went by that he didn't tell someone how glad he was that God instantly healed him of alcoholism. Some people can drink without ruining their lives, but Percy was not in that group. By middle age, Percy was in deep trouble and he knew it. Unfortunately, he was hopelessly addicted. Alcohol was destroying his marriage, his family relationships, and his career.

One day he stood at his kitchen sink and cried out to God. He walked away from the sink a free man. When I met him 30 years later, he was still free, rejoicing in his intact marriage, the love of people around him, and the merciful God who rescued him in an instant. Percy was one of the nicest and happiest people I've ever met. He constantly told people about the God who rescued him.

Unfortunately, it's not always like that. Sometimes people never experience the healing they long for (at least while they are alive).

Between these two human experiences of instantaneous healing and lifelong suffering lie many profound mysteries.

Sometimes healing evades a person

Paul was a leader in the early church. He had lots of experience praying for people and he had seen many people healed. A physician named Luke writes about him:

God did extraordinary miracles through Paul, so that when the handkerchiefs or aprons that had touched his skin were brought to the sick, their diseases left them, and the evil spirits came out of them.[1]

That's pretty good! But in spite of this level of gifting, Paul wrote to Timothy:

Trophimus I left ill in Miletus.[2]

Power for healing flowed through Paul, yet when Trophimus got sick, Paul was unable to do anything about it.

What should you do if you haven't experienced the healing you long for? This chapter and the three that follow it will provide some ideas if you, like Trophimus, are left behind because healing evades you. The purpose of this chapter is to give you hope if you asked God for healing and:

* Things got worse.

* Things remained the same.

* Things improved, but not totally.

There are examples of each in the Bible.

Sometimes things have to get worse before they get better

On rare occasions when people pray, things get worse. The book of Exodus tells the story of a group of slaves. God told Moses to ask the ruler of the land for a three-day holiday for the slaves. The ruler of the land denied Moses' request and ordered that the slaves work *even harder* and be punished *even more severely* for having had the courage to ask for time off. The immediate result of Moses obeying God was increased suffering for the people he was trying to help.[3]

The slaves didn't know it at the time, but their suffering was not to last. Within a year, all the slaves would be free – not for three days, but forever. To get to that desired end, however, they had to endure greater hardship.

Sometimes things have to get worse before they can get better, and withdrawal symptoms are often quite painful. If things have gotten worse for you after you have asked God for help, it is not *necessarily* a bad sign. Keep holding your condition before God who loves you. When things get worse, it *is* a warning, however, that you should recheck all the things you are doing.

* Are you going through the healthy process of withdrawal from something that is not good for you?

* Or is your condition deteriorating?

* Is your diet healthy?

* Are your thought patterns healthy? (It is hard to maintain healthy thought patterns if you're in pain, but this chapter gives some advice.)

* Are there solutions you haven't tried?

* Are there behaviors you need to abandon?

* Are there people who overcame your situation that you could learn from?

* Are there experts you haven't yet consulted?

* If you didn't have this illness, what would you want to do? How can you make some version of that activity possible in spite of your illness?

* How can you have positive experiences in spite of your condition?

Moses no doubt did a lot of soul-searching when things got worse for the people he was trying to help. But since he knew he was on the right course, he persisted and saw victory.

If things have gotten worse for you, it may be a sign that freedom is on its way. Alternatively, it might be a wake-up call that you need an even stronger level of help than you have been getting so far. Get the best advice you can in such situations. Find people who have recovered from your condition and get their advice. Also seek out recognized experts in medicine, in nutrition, in healing prayer and in experimental therapies and get their advice. Ask about their success rates as well as the costs and benefits of the procedures they recommend. Costs include discomfort, downtime, and unexpected consequences.

If nothing changes, persist in prayer

Fortunately, most of the time when people pray their situation does not get worse. But sometimes people pray and find that nothing changes. (The next three chapters will address specific strategies for those times.)

God told Elijah to announce that as punishment for a nation's bad behavior there would be a drought. No rain fell for 36 months. Finally God told Elijah to tell the king that the end of the drought was at hand. Elijah told the king, "Go up, eat and drink, for there is a sound of rushing rain." This was a prophetic statement; at the time there was no evidence that anything had shifted in the weather. Then Elijah started praying for the rain he had predicted. After praying, he told his servant to look for clouds.

The report came back, "There is nothing." Elijah prayed again and sent his servant a second time – and a third time – and a fourth – and a fifth – and a sixth. Each time, nothing.

Sometimes after we pray we can see no physical evidence to support our hope for a different future. In Elijah's case, the change was underway, but it wasn't yet visible. It takes time to reverse a three-year pattern. Finally, the seventh time the servant was told to go look, he could see a tiny change.

"A little cloud, no bigger than a person's hand, is rising out of the sea," he said. Elijah had the servant quickly find the king and warn him to flee in his chariot before torrential rains prevented travel.[4] Elijah recognized the tiny change was a sign of far greater things to come.

Sometimes healing is like that – there is initially no sign that anything is happening. When the first evidence appears, it may seem small and insignificant. But it is worth celebrating. In Elijah's case, once things started to change, they changed quickly. The sky filled with black clouds, the wind rose, and suddenly a fierce rain was pelting the dried out desert. Some cases of healing are like that – no evidence of any progress for months or years and then sudden recovery.

In another story in the Bible, Daniel was told by an angel that God had said yes to one of his prayers *the moment he prayed* – but it took the angel 21 days of fighting to get to Daniel to let him know.[5] Sometimes there are delays but the thing we have desired is on its way.

Keep praying, and don't lose heart

If you have prayed for something and not received an answer, Jesus encourages you to keep asking. Jesus told two stories about this. One of the stories was about the need "to pray always and not to lose heart."[6] In the story, a corrupt judge kept refusing a widow who was asking for justice. But she kept asking. Finally the judge decided, "Though I have no fear of God and no respect for anyone, yet because this widow keeps bothering me, I will grant her justice, so that she may not wear me out by continually coming." Jesus said if an unjust judge could behave like that, "Will not God grant justice to his chosen ones who cry to him day and night? Will he delay long in helping them? I tell you, he will quickly grant justice to them."[7]

Sometimes it seems like prayers for justice or healing are

unheard. But Jesus says to persist – and if you are able to combine persistent prayer with positive action like Dr. Martin Luther King, Jr. did, so much the better.

The other story Jesus tells about persisting in prayer is similar. In this case the characters are two men. One goes to the other's house after midnight to borrow food for company that has just arrived. The lights of his friend's house are out, the door is locked, everyone is sleeping, and no one wants to get up to help the man. But Jesus says, "I tell you, even though [the man's friend] will not get up and give him anything because he is his friend, at least <u>because of his persistence he will get up and give him whatever he needs</u>. So I say to you, Ask, and it will be given you; search, and you will find; knock, and the door will be opened for you."[8]

Ask for God's solution to your problem

Besides persisting, it may be helpful to check your motives. James says in a letter to early Christians that some people don't get answers to their prayers because their motives are selfish.[9] For the most part, this advice does not apply to prayers for healing, since God desires that all people be saved[10] and wants people and the nations to be healed.[11] If you're praying for healing, persist! It's not selfish. But it may be helpful to ask God to purify your motives.

You can also make sure that your request is for something good. God only gives us good things, so if we persist in asking for something bad, we're not going to receive it from God. But if your motives are good and your request is for something good, keep asking. (I keep asking even if my motives are mixed – I know God can sort it all out.)

Perhaps you don't think you would *ever* ask for something bad.

Sometimes people accidentally ask for bad things when they identify specific solutions they want instead of asking for God's solution. For example, a person who is bored might decide the solution was a large screen television.

Perhaps if the person was unable to get out of bed, this would be a realistic solution. But in most cases, the best solution to boredom is not television!

Let's imagine that the person doesn't realize this, so the person begs God for the money and scrimps and saves, and it takes forever. Or maybe the person just buys a television on credit, adding many dollars of interest to the purchase price.

(Buying on credit is like going to a store and bargaining to pay *far more* than the asking price. If you thought about it, you wouldn't want to do that!)

While the person was focused on the television, God would be trying to give that person an exciting purpose for life that would give opportunities for adventure. God's solution would be filled with challenge and joy and unexpected delight.

If the bored person insisted that the only solution was a television, the person would be disappointed with the apparent lack of answers to prayer. (And the person might be irritated at the constant interruption of adventurous opportunities.) But if the person held the boredom before God (the problem, instead of the solution), the person would quickly find the excitement level in life rising – maybe to the point that the excitement seemed "out of control" compared to what the person was used to. Boredom would be a thing of the past.

Let our creative God create what you need

Another example of people holding on to particular solutions is in the area of relationships. Sometimes people say, "God, I won't be content unless that particular person is my spouse." God can see that person's character and knows whether the person would be a good match. I've had people tell me they *had* to get married in a hurry because the other person was so perfect and they just couldn't wait. In three different cases, the couples were divorced within six months. Did the spouses change that much in half a year? Or did they just have aspects of their characters that God could see but their significant others could not?

(Please notice that I am not cautioning against short engagements. I've known at least two where the marriages have lasted decades, and I'm sure there are many others. Instead, I'm talking about cases where one party thinks the other is perfect and that there are no possible problems with the relationship because things are "so good." I've never seen such illusions or such marriages last.)

Instead of telling God the only solution we'll accept, it is much better to hold the problem before God and see how God solves it. God, who created a universe as beautiful and diverse as ours, can come up with beautiful and creative solutions to your problems, too.

To accept God's solution, you might have to be more open than you have been in the past. You might not have recognized a solution because it was so different from what you were imagining. God's solution to your loneliness might not be a spouse. It might be to surround you with orphans who need your love and compassion. Or to place you in a community that can draw out your gifts and help you to grow. Along the way, as you expand and grow, you might find a wonderful spouse, too. Or you might not. In any case, you wouldn't get married because you were lonely. Whatever your problem, it's far better to offer the *problem* to God than a particular solution you have chosen.

Persist in prayer, but do something different

In addition to persisting in prayer, there are two other strategies you can try if nothing has changed. They both relate to trying something new.

Michele Weiner-Davis is a therapist who once recommended divorce to clients that were stuck in their marriages. Not any more. Many factors helped Michele change her mind. Perhaps most important, she found that divorce didn't make things better for her clients. She says after the divorce many people told her they found they were wrong about their ex-spouse being the problem. They had the same problems in their new relationships and even in their lives as single people.

When Michele realized that divorces did not solve the core problems, she took another look at saving marriages. She discovered something amazing: Almost any situation can be improved. Even bad marriages. (Michele's book *Divorce Busting* is worth consulting if you need help improving your marriage.[10] She also has a terrific book of strategies for general problems called *Change Your Life And Everyone In It*.) Michele's strategies are wonderfully helpful and more thorough than I can describe here. But some of her advice can be boiled down to two ideas:

> * Do what works.

> * If what you're doing is not working, do something else.

Michele's first piece of advice is often overlooked by people who are focused on a problem. With their eyes on what's wrong, they don't consider what causes some days to go better than others. When you have a good day, what makes it good? What leads up to it? Do more of that!

One might think Michele's second piece of advice would also be unnecessary. But many people persist in doing what doesn't work. They think if they keep on for a longer time, or with more effort, or with more volume, things will change. Michele's advice can set us free: If it hasn't worked in the past, it's not likely to work in the future. Try something else.

The classic example of this is someone who wants something done, so they ask their spouse to do it. Nothing happens within a desired time frame. So they ask again. Nothing happens. They ask again – perhaps not as nicely. Years later, they still may be begging or nagging, even though they have years of experience that such strategies aren't effective.

If a particular technique hasn't produced the desired results, why keep using it? Try something else. It really doesn't matter if you think your strategy *should* be successful. If it is not, do something different. Keep varying your approach until you find something that works.

Excel in spite of your condition

Anna Mary Robertson grew up on a farm. She married a farmer at age 27. In their 40-year marriage they had 10 children, five of whom died in infancy. Anna loved to embroider – but she reached a point where arthritis made it too painful. In her seventies, she switched to painting and completed more than 2,000 scenes of the rural farm life of her childhood.

Although she never got relief from arthritis, the disease propelled her to the career for which she has become known. Her marriage to Thomas Moses and her farm career impacted only a few people in New England. But her paintings have been seen and loved by millions around the world. Ironically, Grandma Moses would never have completed so many paintings if she had not gotten arthritis.

Sometimes if you pray for healing and nothing happens, a courageous spirit can help you rise above your condition in ways that bless hundreds, thousands, or millions. If you have not yet seen the complete healing you seek, find people who have recovered from your condition and ask what they did. But in the meantime, ask God for a way to transcend your condition that brings blessing to others.

Sometimes people get better in stages

Sometimes after people pray, things improve, but not

completely. Once Jesus prayed for a man who was blind. Jesus spit on the man's eyes and laid his hands on him. Then Jesus asked the man if he could see anything. The man reported he could now see people but they looked like trees walking.

I'm not sure how to picture that – except that clearly the man's vision wasn't yet perfect. His sight was improved, but it was not yet normal. Jesus put his hands on the man's eyes a second time. At that point the man began to see clearly.[11]

If Jesus had to pray twice for something, we shouldn't be surprised if sometimes we have to pray more than once. Sometimes (like Jesus) we'll see partial results and we'll need to pray again. Other times we'll see no results but feel like God wants us to persist. It's worth it in those times to persevere.

Persisting doesn't mean you'll always get what you are asking for. Paul had what he called a thorn in his flesh. He begged God to take away. He asked three times but God finally told him, "My grace is sufficient for you, for power is made perfect in weakness."[12] That realization gave Paul the courage to embrace his weakness. But notice the order: don't embrace your weakness until *after* you have repeatedly asked God to take care of it and God has told you "No!"

Once you've discovered the solution, it will seem easy

Sometimes people have to embrace their weaknesses for the rest of their lives. Other times it is only for a season. If you are opening a safe and correctly spin the dial to the first two numbers, the safe will not open yet. It needs the full combination. Even though you've done everything correctly so far, it doesn't count until the full combination is entered. Healing some conditions is like this. You may have several of the essentials, but still need one or two more things to fall into place.

Some time ago, I checked into a hotel in Hawaii. The room was way too hot when I arrived. I had to stand on a chair to reach the air conditioner, which was bolted above the door frame. Stretching, I pushed the button marked, "Cool." Nothing. I pushed "Cool – max." Nothing. I flipped switches, I turned dials, and pushed more buttons. Still nothing. The air conditioner just didn't work.

I was going to be in Hawaii five days. If this air conditioner didn't work, it was going to be a very uncomfortable stay.

You may find this silly, but I prayed for the air conditioner. As soon as I finished praying, I noticed a light switch on the wall behind me. I flipped the light switch. The air conditioner roared to life.

There was no sign on the light switch that said "air conditioner" or "try this." The switch wasn't close enough to the air conditioner to suggest a connection between the two. Similarly, the solution to your healing may not have a sign on it, and the connection to your healing may not be obvious yet. Once you discover the solution, it will probably seem quite simple. But until you find it, you can poke all the buttons and dials and switches you want and nothing's going to happen.

Many illnesses are directly linked to emotional conditions that seem unrelated. People often are healed when they finally give up what they thought was an unconnected condition like resentment, bitterness or a critical spirit.[13] If you haven't been healed yet, you might ask yourself what parts of your personality make you less fun to be around. Try giving some of those up, even though you think they are justified. The worst that can happen is that your friendships will improve! But you might also find that one of them works like that "unrelated" light switch in Hawaii.

Once you've discovered a solution, you'll find it often works in other settings. The next time I'm in a hotel room with an air conditioner that doesn't work, I'll look for a light switch. But I didn't think of it the first time around because I'd never seen that arrangement before.

There *is* a solution to your problem. You may not have discovered it yet, but there is a solution.

Many times people were healed by the power of Jesus with a word, even after a lifetime of illness:

* Jesus healed a man who had been lame for 38 years.[14]

* Jesus healed a woman who had been bleeding 12 years.[15]

* Jesus' disciples also healed people who had been sick for years, even raising people from the dead.[16]

Jesus' power to heal continues to this day. One example is Percy, mentioned at the start of this chapter, who was healed of alcoholism instantly. For people who are not yet well, in the next three chapters we'll discuss how you can be healed:

* with a process.

* with a change.

* at the end.

Checklist

_____   Ask God for help.

_____   If things get worse, review the diagnostic questions on page 53.

_____   Thank God for any small positive changes.

_____   Persist.

_____   Ask God to help your motivation flow from God's love.

_____   Ask God for God's solution.

_____   Do more of what works.

_____   Find people who have recovered from your condition and find out what they did.

_____   If something's not working, quit doing it and try something else.

_____   Rise above your condition like Grandma Moses did.

Questions for Discussion

1) Have you ever had a situation you prayed about get worse? What happened?

2) How can you tell the difference between withdrawal symptoms from a poison (a positive event) and a deteriorating condition?

3) What kind of withdrawal symptoms might there be from poisonous activities like resentment, gossip, jealousy, or rage?

4) Are there any questions you would add to the list on page 53 of things to check when things get worse?

5) Have you ever had a situation you prayed about remain unchanged? What did you do?

6) Is it easy for you to "pray always and not lose heart"?[17] What encourages you to keep praying?

7) Do you tend to ask God for particular solutions that you have identified? Or do you ask God to come up with the solutions?

8) What is something you haven't tried yet that has worked for other people?

9) What would be a way you could transcend your condition, like Grandma Moses did when she began painting?

10) What are some stuck situations that you've seen change overnight, like when Elijah prayed for rain?

11) What else in this chapter caught your attention?

Chapter 6

You Can Be Healed With A Process

Once I had what was officially diagnosed as a "fever of unknown origin." Unfortunately for me, right before I got this fever I moved to a town that was 100 degrees. I had a black car with no air conditioning. Because of the illness, my heart was racing and I lost too much weight to be healthy. I had a continual headache and I had almost no physical energy. The doctor said whatever I had wasn't contagious, so I drove to work two days a week, baking in my superheated car. That was all I had the strength to do. Before the illness I had been able to run for thirty minutes to an hour. After the fever hit, I got to where I only had enough energy to walk half a block before I collapsed. I had to carefully ration my steps.

After some time went by, I could walk a whole block. At that point, I had to keep reminding myself that I was getting better. I was *twice as good* as I had been. It was hard to remember, however, since I was so far from where I wanted to be.

Sometimes a person's healing is progressing so slowly that it is hard to recognize. It is hard to keep hope in such times, but doing so will help, and it is appropriate for the situation.

Persist!

Sometimes people who are ill are required to persist – to endure a slow process of recovery before they experience the healing they desire. Jesus told a story of a foreigner who found a man beaten by robbers.[1] The hero of the story did not pray that the man's wounds would be suddenly healed. Instead he cleaned them, bandaged them, and provided someone to care for the wounded man throughout the length of his recuperation. When telling the story, Jesus instructed his followers to "go and do likewise" – to help people through long periods of recovery, to expend their time and resources on those around them who need help, to treat hurting people as if they were beloved neighbors.

In some cases – like the case of the man beaten by robbers – healing occurs over the course of days, weeks or months. Or years. My mom had to have a pacemaker soon after they were invented. At that time they were the size of a pack of cigarettes. The batteries didn't last and the units had to be replaced every two or three years, a painful surgery with a long recuperation time. My mom had her chest opened five times in four years.

When she left for her first surgery, some people didn't believe she was going to come back. Her heart rate had fallen to about 30 beats a minute.

The day after the pacemaker was installed, its probes slipped out of place, and the team had to reopen her chest to position the probes correctly. The hospital where this took place was 600 miles from our home in Alaska. Mom was gone from September through early December.

When she finally got home, she was bedridden most of the day. She kept this hidden from us as much as possible. She would get up to see us off to school and then return to bed until 3 p.m. At three, when we got out of school, she would get up until 7 p.m., when she would go back to bed. She only had enough energy to be up five hours a day.

During the long time of healing when Mom had no strength to cook, people from the Lutheran church we belonged to brought dinners to our family every night. They also prayed. Every week the local Baptist minister prayed for Mom on his radio show. Every morning children at the Roman Catholic school included Mom in their prayers. The mercy of people outside our immediate circle of friends was encouraging. Progress was slow but, after months, there was progress. Eventually Mom had the strength to cook. Eventually she had the strength to go back to work half time.

Two years later, because the battery was worn out, Mom had to go through the surgery again. Again the second day they had to reopen her chest and reposition the probes.

But eventually my mom's heart became whole. She recovered to where she didn't need the pacemaker at all. Her healing was gradual, but it was welcome when it arrived. When Mom went to the hospital to have the pacemaker taken out for good, the nurse didn't believe such a thing was possible. "Oh, no, dearie," she said. "You're just here to have your batteries changed." Fortunately, that was not the case.

Looking back, Mom's healing was miraculous. But living through it, one slow day at a time, it did not seem like a miracle. "It was very discouraging at times," Mom said. "I couldn't do what I wanted to do." When she complained to her doctor about her lack of progress, he said he didn't know if she *would* get better. He told her she got the pacemaker to see if it would help, not as a promise that she would recover.

This chapter is for people who have seen some recovery, but it has been slight (and might even be overlooked unless you pay close attention). In such cases, twelve points of advice may aid the recovery that is slowly going on:

1) Keep seeking the best medical help you can get.

2) Get all the prayer you can from others.

3) Pray regularly for yourself

4) Ask questions that lead to outcomes you desire.

5) Listen to your intuitions.

6) Regularly take time to be thankful for all that is good in your life.

7) Resolve emotional pain.

8) Don't give up on processes that work.

9) Do things to benefit others.

10) Laugh all you can.

11) Get to know God better.

12) Keep track of your recovery in a journal.

The rest of this chapter will discuss these twelve points.

Get the best help possible

1) Keep seeking the best medical help you can get.

The advice you need may be farther away than you've looked so far. You or a friend can check medical reference books in libraries and search the internet for people who have recovered from your condition and for solutions that work. You are worth it!

2) Get all the prayer you can from others.

Go to churches that specialize in healing prayer and have people pray for you. If you cannot get out, call such churches and ask to be included in their prayers. Then spend time each day thanking God for the healing power God is sending you.

3) Pray regularly for yourself.

Place your hand on the impacted area and ask God's healing power to flow through your hand. Imagine God's love and compassion flowing into your body and surrounding the impacted area.

Our minds tend to figure out how to accomplish the things we hold before them on a regular basis. That is why it is helpful to stay focused on health, picturing yourself well.

Ask questions that lead to outcomes you desire

4) Ask questions that lead to outcomes you desire.

Stay focused on health. Ask yourself:

> * "What can I do today to help me recover?"
>
> * "What good happened last week and how will I celebrate it?"
>
> * "What good events can I schedule for next week and how can I make them happen?"
>
> * "If I were well, what would be my ultimate goal?"
>
> * "How can I move toward that goal this week?"

Unfortunately, many times people ask questions that lead *away* from what they want. Sometimes people ask, "Why am I so sick?" The question is okay to ask once, to give you ideas of what to change. But it's not a question you want to dwell on! If you do, your brain will come up with reasons for you to stay sick. How much better to ask, "What can I do to become more healthy?"

If at first you don't have any answers to positive questions, persist. Eventually your brain will come up with wonderfully creative paths towards anything you hold before it.

Listen to your intuitions
as well as your rational guesses

5) Listen to your intuitions.

Your intuitive side has access to information you may not be consciously aware of. It often reports information in dreams and visual symbols packed with meaning. These may seem random until they are correctly interpreted.

A young girl was once brought to Dr. Bernie Siegel because she had enlarged lymph nodes in her neck and jaw. Her parents had lymphoma in both their families, so they were worried. While working with this girl, Bernie had her make some drawings. She drew herself and her family's cat. The beautiful drawing of the cat showed claws on each of its paws. Bernie writes:

> As I stared at her drawing, wondering why this cat was such a vivid presence to her at a time when she was so sick, it suddenly dawned on me that she had cat scratch fever.[2]

Tests showed that Bernie's hunch was correct, and that the girl was free of lymphoma.

It is unlikely that the young girl had the medical background to consciously know the cause of her illness. But her subconscious mind knew. Fortunately, she was being treated by a doctor who could decode the clues her drawings provided.

If you have a vivid dream, ask God to help you decode the symbols and discover what it means. The clues provided by our subconscious mind are rarely presented in a straightforward way. This makes them harder to recognize. But God can give you insight into their meaning. If you can't figure it out, some charismatic churches have people with prophetic insight into interpreting dreams. Call one in your area to see if they can help.

Use your imagination to picture yourself well

Ideally, communication with the right side of your brain will be two-way. Besides listening to your intuitions and dreams, fill your imagination with pictures of what you want to accomplish. Sports stars, business leaders, and people of many other backgrounds often use their imaginations to rehearse what they want to happen.

Researchers believe the brain cannot tell the difference between something imagined in great detail and something experienced. As a result, many think the mind can be programmed towards desired behavior by vividly picturing what you want.[3] Sports greats picture themselves making perfect plays over and over. Follow their example and picture yourself well. Imagine yourself actively doing what is not yet possible. It will help guide your subconscious mind to find the solutions you desire.

Fortunately, this is an exercise you can do no matter how weak you feel! Try it for five minutes, three times a day, picturing yourself doing all the things you want to do when you are well.

6) *Regularly take time to be thankful for all that is good in your life.*

Another way to actively use your mind and imagination to stay focused on health was mentioned at the start of this chapter: Be thankful for improvements you have already seen, no matter how small, and call them to mind on a regular basis. If you're praying for rain as Elijah was and you see a little cloud no bigger than a person's hand on the distant horizon, praise God for it.[4] The event may not look like much, but after three years of no rain, to have a cloud rise out of the sea is *a big deal*, even if it is still far away and seems like it may have no impact on you. When we thank God for tiny amounts of progress, it puts us in a position to receive more.

**People can receive healing
even if they reject it at first**

7) *Resolve emotional pain.*

Naaman was the skilled commander of the army of the nation

of Aram. His king respected him highly because he was so successful in battle, even though Naaman had leprosy. Leprosy was a dreaded disease that caused people of his day to be social outcasts. One day, Naaman captured a young girl who said he could be cured by Elisha, an Israeli prophet. When Naaman heard this, he set out with an offering for Elisha: 750 pounds of silver, 150 pounds of gold and ten sets of clothing. (Given the extravagance of the offering, you can see how successful he must have been – and how desperate for healing!)

After a long journey, Naaman arrived at Elisha's house. Elisha refused to come out. Instead, he sent a servant to tell Naaman, "Go, wash in the Jordan seven times, and your flesh shall be restored and you shall be clean."

At first Naaman was furious that the prophet wouldn't see him – and also that he had been told to do something he could have done in his own country. But eventually his servants prevailed. They told him, "If the prophet had commanded you to do something difficult, would you not have done it? How much more, when all he said to you was, 'Wash, and be clean'?"[5]

I have a guess what was going on. It's only a guess: The text simply doesn't say. But the text does say that Naaman was a leper. In Israel, lepers were required to shout "Unclean!" whenever they approached, so people could avoid them. Perhaps the social rules in Naaman's home country of Aram were similar. Even if they were not, leprosy was a feared disease that left people horribly disfigured.

As a result of Naaman's skill and rank, he had no doubt been able to avoid *some* of the reproach of his disease. But he must also have known rejection. He must have had people who avoided his presence. He must have had others who didn't avoid him but couldn't bear to look at the places where the disease was affecting his skin. And he must have had others who couldn't take their eyes *off* his disfigurement. He must have faced years of misery and rejection over a condition he himself did not cause.

Resolving emotional pain sometimes brings healing

I am guessing that when Elisha refused to see him, it brought to the surface all the years of rejection from dozens or hundreds (or maybe even thousands) of people. It had been bad enough that *they* had rejected him. But now even the representative of *God* wouldn't come near him!

I'm guessing that Elisha's refusal to be in Naaman's presence brought to the surface Naaman's anger and resentment over his condition and his fear that God had abandoned him. I think that is why he was so angry that he was ready to leave without trying to be healed.

As I said, it's just a guess. All I can say for sure is that when other people have gotten over resentment, bitterness or fear, many have experienced physical healing that same day.

You can move closer to physical healing by resolving emotional pain in your life. This can be done by taking three simple steps:

* Have mercy on people who have wronged you and forgive them. (They don't deserve it. This is not about justice, it's about you becoming more loving.)

* Make amends for wrongs you have done that still grieve you or others.

* Act as if you were filled with love, ceasing activities that don't fit with that new self-image, and taking on new activities that do. (This step alone will bring a transformation; peace and joy will start to flow into your life.)

**Sometimes results aren't visible
until the end of the process**

8) Don't give up on processes that work.

In Naaman's case, he finally listened to the advice of his servants and went down to the Jordan River. He splashed into the water once and came out. Nothing had changed. Twice. The leprosy was the same as before. Three times. There was no sign that what he was doing having any effect. Four times, in and out. By then he was probably cold and wondering if the prophet just wanted to make him look like a fool. Five times into the water and back out. Nothing. Six times. No sign of a change. Since it wasn't working, should he give up? Should he quit and go home?

Fortunately for Naaman, that's not what he did. After the sixth time, he may have been discouraged and he may have *felt* like quitting. He may even have lost hope, since nothing had changed so far. But he got back in the water one last time. And the story says that when he came out, something remarkable happened. His skin was changed. He was well.[6]

Perhaps the seven cold-water baths gave Naaman the time to completely release his spirit from bitterness and anger over his disease and the rejection he had encountered. The story doesn't say *why* the seven baths were effective. But they were.

Naaman's story is instructive because the change occurred all at once after a process where it appeared that nothing was happening. Naaman's cure required that he walk through the entire process *before* seeing any results.

When Naaman first heard the message of Elisha's servant, he was ready to go home without trying to be healed. Like Naaman, many people are within sight of a cure but they reject it because they don't like how it is packaged or what it entails. Others start out following good advice but don't see any results, so they quit too early. And others see results, think they are cured, and stop doing what was healing them. Hopefully if that's true for you, you'll have friends like Naaman's servants, who convinced him to keep going.

Naaman's cure required him to persist through the entire

process.

Unfortunately, some processes *never* work, no matter how long you stick with them. If you're persisting with a process, you should do some research. How many people get better by following the process? Of the people who got better, what percent showed no improvement for a while before they got better? How long did it take before their improvement started? How does that compare with your results?

Elisha's advice wasn't effective simply because it was odd. It was effective because it was from God. The story suggests that if someone *with a proven track record* gives you odd sounding advice, you may want to follow it.[7]

Help others while you are waiting for recovery

9) Do things to benefit others.

Steve Sjogren was the pastor of a tiny church in Cincinnati. The church grew to more than 6,000 after Steve began teaching the congregation to do small acts of kindness to show God's love to people. While this exciting ministry was developing, Steve went to the hospital for a simple surgery. His aorta was accidentally punctured twice in the procedure. He says, "I basically had a major stroke and I bled to death on the operating table. They put 50-some units of blood [into me] trying to get my blood pressure up."[8] Before the doctors could figure out what was wrong, Steve suffered severe neurological damage. At a talk he gave six years after the procedure, Steve was still not fully recovered, although he continued to lead a dynamic congregation.

Shortly after the operation, people would visit Steve in the hospital and ask what they could do for him. Steve asked them to help him into his wheelchair. Then they would go down to the Popsicle machine and buy as many Popsicles as they could afford. They took the red, green and purple Popsicles to people in the hospital and offered them a choice of color and taste.

People in a hospital have few choices that are beautiful, colorful, delightful or fun. The simple act of offering Popsicles to people in that setting is a brilliant idea.

Note that Steve was doing this before he was able to walk, before he felt good, and before he had any guarantees that he himself would recover from the devastating effects of his surgery.

After Steve had progressed to being able to walk, he went back to visiting neighbors to show them God's love through simple acts of kindness – often by volunteering to clean their toilets, something he had done before his surgery.

More than six years after the surgery, many tasks were still physically impossible for Steve. He still had trouble going up and down stairs. The slow pace of his recovery was not due to lack of prayer. It was not due to lack of medical help. Some conditions are difficult to treat. But in the midst of his physical challenges, Steve continued to help others. If you follow Steve's example in this, you will find your spirits lifted, even if your body does not improve as much as you'd like. Having a heart of generosity is remarkably healing to one's emotional system.

Six years into his recovery, Steve said, "I'm at the point where I realize I can't do big things any longer. . . . All I can really do is small things over and over again consistently. . . . [But] I think when you add up all the small steps, they become a big thing in the name of Christ."

Steve cites the example of Mother Teresa, who once said her best accomplishment was carrying 35,000 dead and dying people from the gutters of Calcutta, India, to a hospice where they could die in dignity. Asked what her greatest discovery was, she said, "If I wouldn't have carried the first person in, I wouldn't have carried the 35,000[th] person in." A lot of small steps can take a person quite a ways. All we have to do is take the first small step. And then another.

Laugh all you can

10) Laugh all you can.

Decades ago, Norman Cousins discovered the healing benefits of laughter. He found laughing helped him manage pain as he recovered from cancer. Norman watched comedies as part of his self-imposed therapy. Perhaps this form of therapy will help you as well. (It certainly won't hurt!)

Laughter frees our spirits to be more receptive to creative ideas. If you're having trouble thinking of solutions to advance your own healing, you may have grown too serious (a predictable event when dealing with a stubborn, unwanted condition!). Find a way to get your mind onto something that makes you laugh.

Find out how much God loves you

11) Get to know God better.

Some people do not know that God loves them. Once people believe God loves them at their emotional core, many people find their problems melt away — either becoming insignificant or disappearing entirely.

You get to know God better the same way you get to know other friends: you hang out with them doing nothing, you work with them on projects, you play with them in recreation time, you talk to them about what's on your mind, and you express appreciation for who they are. If you want to know God better, do the same kinds of things:

> * read the Bible and reflect on it. Sometimes people find it helpful to meditate several times a day on specific verses that seem to apply to them. One friend recommends treating a helpful verse like a prescription for medicine: "Meditate on this verse once every four hours, thinking about how it related to the past four hours and how you might apply it in the next four."

* work with others on things God cares about.

* find ways to delight in God and in creation.

* talk to God about anything you're thinking about. Pay attention to impressions and new ideas that come to you.

* express appreciation to God for who God is.

Track your progress

12) Keep track of your recovery in a journal.

Studies have shown that writing memories and emotions in a journal often sets people free. You may also find encouragement from recording your prayers and their answers as well as your daily thoughts.

Checklist

_____   Be grateful for positive changes, however small.

_____   Persist.

_____   Get great medical advice.

_____   Get ongoing prayer.

_____   Ask questions that lead to outcomes you desire.

_____   Listen to your intuitions and dreams for clues of how to become healthy.

_____   Use your imagination to picture yourself active and well.

_____   Resolve emotional pain.

_____   Forgive everyone who has wronged you.

_____   Make amends for wrongs you have done.

_____   Act as if you were filled with love.

_____   Don't give up on processes that work.

_____   Do things to benefit others.

_____   Laugh all you can.

_____   Get to know God better.

_____   Keep track of your thoughts and progress in a journal.

Questions for Discussion

1) What conditions do you have that seem stuck? Have you seen <u>any</u> progress? (Small changes count!)

2) Are you currently involved with the long-term care of someone? If so, what help do you need?

3) If not, have you ever cared for someone long term? What was helpful to you in that instance?)

4) What questions can you ask that will lead to outcomes you desire?

5) What clues about solutions have you gotten from intuitions and dreams? What dreams and intuitions still need to be decoded? Who can help you with that?

6) Picture yourself well for five or ten minutes, three times a day, for a week. What does that feel like?

7) Have you ever received odd sounding advice from someone with a proven track record? Did you accept or reject that advice? What happened?

8) Naaman had to wash to be healed. Perhaps he needed to wash away his disappointment and resentment. What emotional pain do you have that needs to be washed away?

9) What are ways you can follow Steve Sjogren's example of helping others through simple actions?

10) What comedies cause you to laugh out loud? When will you watch them?

11) What will you do to get to know God better?

12) What else in this chapter caught your attention?

Chapter 7

You Can Be Healed With A Change

Can you take pictures with a lens cap covering your camera's lens? For many cameras, the answer is yes. The pictures just won't turn out. You may have the aperture set correctly, the focus right, the shutter speed right, and the right recording media or film in the camera. The camera may be fully operational, with a fresh battery. You may be looking at a scene that is breathtaking, with the camera pointed in the right direction to capture everything perfectly. And if the lens cap is on, none of that will matter. You won't get a usable image.

Sometimes there are simple things we need to do before we can get the results we desire. Everything else may be in place, but something is blocking the results we want. In such cases, it's good to ask God for help in identifying hidden blocks.

If an alcoholic wants a job or money, better relationships or more possessions, a prayer team can pray with the person for any of those and the alcoholic may receive them. But the answer to prayer may be short-lived if the root problem is not dealt with. The real problem wasn't employment or wages or people or possessions. Bad choices brought on by the alcoholic haze caused the loss of these. The root problem needs to be dealt with. (And in this example, the root problem may not be alcohol. It may be a poor self image, pride, indifference, prejudice, anger, weakness, or some other condition.) Ask God to reveal the root issue and help you take care of it.

**You can help expose the real issue by asking,
"Why do I need this illness?"**

One question that may help you identify the root cause is a little shocking to some people when they first hear it. I was taught the question at a hospital that had their chaplains ask each patient, "Why do you need this illness?"

Many patients were surprised by the question. Most took it pretty well, but people who *aren't* hospitalized sometimes get angry when they first hear it. The question implies a level of responsibility that many people don't want to accept. Inside the hospital, however, I've seen many people gain tremendous insight when they consider the question. Sometimes people realize their illness is a call to avoid certain activities or substances or people that are toxic to them. Other times the question helps people realize a connection between their illness and aspects of their lives that they want to amend.

As I talked to people in the hospital, I heard lots of stories. I didn't recognize the pattern of the stories, however, until I was talking with a woman who had experienced a heart attack.

Another helpful question is, "What was happening before I got sick?"

"I can't understand why this happened," she said. "I've always been so healthy. Before I had the heart attack, I decided to see my sister. She and I always fight; I've hated her as long as I can remember. But I thought it was time we made amends. I was just stepping onto the Greyhound bus to visit her when I had my heart attack. I can't understand it, since I've always had good health. Anyway, as soon as I'm well, I'm going to get back on that bus and go see her."

I had heard story after story like that throughout that summer. But I hadn't seen the pattern. Somehow her story was plain enough so it all came together for me – and I recognized the pattern of the stories of dozens of patients I'd already talked to. This woman's brain may have decided to visit her sister, but her heart clearly wasn't in it. And until she resolved the heart issues, she was probably going to have trouble getting on that bus, no matter what her mind decided.

In this woman's case, she needed her illness because she had told herself for 20 years that she would avoid her sister at all costs. When her brain ordered her body to visit the sister, the heart carried out 20 years of prior orders. As far as her heart knew, those orders had not been revised. Her heart hadn't yet gotten the message – no doubt still in development – that she was going to try a new approach.

(If you are offended by crude language, please skip to the next paragraph.) Illness is often symbolic of the dilemmas of our lives. Many patients I spoke with in the hospital backed up this idea with their stories, often pointing to a direct connection between their illnesses and their lives' events. One man felt he had to stay in his job. Unfortunately, it was highly stressful and involved many negative people trying to control what he did. He was very creative and normally functioned well, but every now and then he lost the ability to handle the negativity. When I saw him, his body had become unable to process waste effectively and his intestinal distress was so severe he had to be hospitalized. "Why do you need this illness?" I asked. He was surprised by the question but knew the answer. "Because I can't take this shit." Seeing the direct link between his inward and outward realities helped him recover physically and gave him clear insight of what he needed to work on in his job to continue to stay healthy. (If you have people trying to control your life and tell you what to do, I highly recommend the book *Boundaries: When to Say Yes, When to Say No to Take Control of Your Life* by Henry Cloud and John Townsend.)

I do not mean to imply that all diseases reflect our lives with such perfect symbolism. But since many do, it is worth considering what links your illness might have with your life. In your case, there may be no link. (I'll talk about an example where that was true later in this chapter.) But it would probably be helpful to talk over these questions with a friend just in case. Sometimes others can see things we overlook.

Answering the question "Why do I need this illness?" may

help you discover attitudes, habits or conditions that need to change before you can get better. Similarly, asking "What was going on before I got sick?" may help you remember conditions that your physical system reacted to.

Sometimes we need to change our behavior before we can be healed

One of the reasons change is sometimes required before we can experience healing is that all of life functions on cause and effect. Sometimes we can't be healed (an effect) until what's causing our disease is dealt with first.

The Bible is quite clear that some behaviors lead to illness or even death. Psalm 107:17 says, "Some were sick through their sinful ways and because of their iniquities endured affliction."[1] Similarly Psalm 38:3b says, "There is no health in my bones because of my sin." James, a follower of Jesus, writes:

> Confess your sins to one another, and pray for one another, so that you may be healed.[2]

If sin is the cause of your illness, it is worth it to change

Unfortunately, the root cause of an illness is often invisible to us. Ask for God's help in identifying the root. People who gossip about others often see nothing wrong with their behavior and don't recognize the link between gossip and their own problems. This is true for many harmful actions, whether they be envy, jealousy, a critical nature, or something else.[3]

Occasionally the root cause is something that was not harmful in the past. In Japan in the 1960s, the people of Minamata were poisoned by fish they were eating. People in the town had eaten fish for centuries without ill effect, but a company had started dumping mercury-laden waste into the bay. The townspeople did not know they were eating poisoned fish. But their lack of knowledge did not shield them from the disastrous results.

Their children were born severely deformed, and once-healthy children and adults lost vision, speech ability, and motor function before collapsing into unconsciousness and death. The company denied involvement even though their own scientist had proven a direct link to the conditions. W. Eugene Smith, a photojournalist documenting the horror, was beaten so severely by thugs from the company that he lost some of his vision in one eye. Eventually the whole town knew the truth, the company stopped polluting the water, and the birth defects ceased. But many children were deformed and many people died before the cause known to everyone. Being ignorant of the poison did not shield people from its effects.

To stay healthy, you have to obey natural law

This illustrates an important rule of cause and effect: Health requires obedience to natural law even if we don't know what that law is. That's why God encouraged the people of Israel to listen carefully to the commandments given for their good.[4]

The Bible is very clear:

1) Disobeying natural law will lead to unhappy consequences, whether you know the law or not.[5]

2) People often do not know or acknowledge the extent of their own responsibility for their condition.[6]

3) When people obey natural law, things go well for them. Amazingly, healing often comes to a vast area when people begin following God's ways. In 2 Chronicles 7:14, God promises: "If my people who are called by my name humble themselves, pray, seek my face, and turn from their wicked ways, then I will hear from heaven, and will forgive their sin and heal their land." Notice what is healed. It is not just the people who turn back to God – it is their whole land!

The Bible is also clear about two more points, which make

everything more complicated:

4) Not all blessing is a result of doing good.[7]

5) Not all tragedy and illness is a result of doing something bad.[8]

In some cases, the cause is outside your field of influence

The Bible has a very large book devoted to the idea that illness isn't always a result of bad behavior. It tells the story of a man named Job. Although Job lived an exemplary life, his children were killed, his businesses collapsed, and Job himself became painfully ill. When three of his friends arrived to console him, they were so devastated by Job's appearance that they couldn't speak. At first. As time went by, however, they made up for their initial silence by telling Job, first politely, then increasingly forcefully, that he must have done something wrong to deserve such tragedies, and he should change at once so he could return to health.

For many people, the advice of those three friends would be exactly what they needed to hear. Many people *have* done things that are wrong (often that they don't recognize) and as soon as they change, they *will* experience better states. In Job's case, however, he had done nothing wrong. All his misfortune happened because of forces outside of Job's control, and the unsound advice of his three friends was one more thing he had to endure. The story of Job ends with a strong rebuke of Job's three friends and the assertion that the presence of an illness does not always mean that sin or bad choices were involved. But before Job is vindicated, his friends talk about his need to change for a long, long time.

Many centuries after the story of Job was written, Jesus was confronted by people who assumed that a particular man was blind because he or his parents sinned. Jesus reaffirmed the teaching of the book of Job, saying that illnesses are not always a result of sin.[9]

One illustration of this is my own experience with headaches.

Sometimes prayers don't help
until you make a change

In college I had headaches. The headaches were painful and lasted 24 hours or more. I could still go to class, but it was difficult to cope since the pain was so great. On days when I had a headache, I had to move slowly to minimize the pain. Exercise was out of the question until the headaches subsided.

During that time, I read a book about food allergies. It said if you have a food allergy, it is relatively easy to discover. The book said all you have to do is list your ten favorite foods – if you're allergic to anything, it'll likely show up in your top ten favorites. I laughed when I read that. I instantly knew what my allergy would be. My top three favorite foods were coffee, chocolate and cola. All contain caffeine. But I wasn't giving those up. I *liked* them. Plus, my headaches weren't that bad.

After college my headaches got worse. I had aspirin containers in the pockets of every jacket, coat, and suit I owned. I got to where my headaches were continual: I had no relief, from the time I got up until I fell asleep at night.

One day my headache was so bad I got desperate: I stopped consuming caffeine, I started eating vegetables I didn't like, I started exercising, and I changed a few other habits. The pain was so bad I was willing to try everything at once in the hope that *something* in the mix would make the pain less. A week later I was attending a talk and the pain so great I left in the middle in tears. I didn't know what I was going to do. Exercise hadn't helped, fresh vegetables hadn't helped, and giving up caffeine hadn't helped. I couldn't stand the pain, and I didn't believe in suicide. How was I going to be able to stand to live?

I got no answer that day. But that is the kind of prayer that

God loves to answer. God listens to the cries of our hearts.

Meanwhile, my one-week experiment of trying to do good things had resulted in even more intense pain. I decided that if I was going to have my headaches anyway, there was no sense giving up foods I liked (coffee, cola and chocolate) and eating foods I didn't like (vegetables). I went back to my former patterns with a vengeance. What did it matter?

But God had heard my prayers.

God can orchestrate coincidences to help you

Some time later, a friend of mine started using drugs. He was in a youth group that I was advising. This friend pursued everything with tremendous energy. When he skied, he was the best – or at least the most daring – and he was like that with whatever he did. He was a great athlete and an awesome guy. When he started using drugs, I guessed he would pursue them with the same fearless abandon with which he approached everything else. I knew he was in danger of messing up his life. I decided to fast for him.

As I was thinking about fasting, I asked myself, "What kind of fast could I do that would be the equivalent of his giving up drugs?" Once I asked the question, it was easy to answer. My giving up caffeine would be just as unexpected as him giving up drugs. I usually drank six to eight cans of cola a day. I ate an eight-ounce bar of chocolate regularly. I drank many cups of coffee a day, often three or four in a row. I loved all those. But I wanted my friend to be free of drugs. So I gave them all up in a fast for his sake.

A month or two later I was pushing a cart down an aisle in a supermarket. I still remember the exact spot in the store where I suddenly realized that for the first time in years I didn't have a headache. At all.

I couldn't believe it. The pain was completely gone.

Eliminate the cause
and the symptoms can disappear

Over the course of the next few months, I discovered that 90% of my headaches were caused by caffeine. The bulk of the rest were caused by sugar. Earlier when I tried to do everything I could to be healthy, I didn't know that it can take two weeks to be free of the effects of caffeine in a person's system. I had made it half way through before giving up in frustration.

After the fast for my friend ended, I experimented. I tried just a small amount of chocolate. Surely a little bit wouldn't matter. (It did.) Surely I could drink decaffeinated coffee without trouble. (I couldn't.) Surely a little cola would be worth it. (It never was.) The 24-hour pain that followed each episode taught me I wanted to stay free of those substances.

Initially, I *longed* for coffee and chocolate and cola. It required hourly discipline to keep reminding myself that the pain wasn't worth it. But over the years my patterns changed. Today I don't miss caffeine and there's no lingering longing. A couple times a year I think wistfully about how I'd get a burst of energy after midnight by drinking lots of coffee. But it's not a strong impulse, and it's never connected with the thought that I should drink some coffee now. The pain is too great. I don't even long for the taste any more, though I know I enjoy it. I choose to like other things that are less painful.

You can benefit from what others have learned

Some of the people who read this account will be suffering from the effects of caffeine. Two weeks after they give it up, they will be freed of their symptoms – headaches (as in my case), excruciating neck pain (as in Jerry Savelle's case, discussed next), or something else. I didn't tell the story specifically for those friends, but they will benefit from the details nonetheless.

A larger group of people will have allergies other than caffeine that are causing various discomforts. Allergic reactions can range from painful physical symptoms to mental states like inattention, apathy, hyperactivity, and the like. Readers who are able to identify and give up their allergens will also greatly benefit from the story.

But I did not tell the story only for people in those groups. Rather, I told it because I believe that *all* readers can benefit from it. Here are some ideas that are applicable to many people:

> * I reached a point of agonizing pain even though I had been trying to follow God all my life.
>
> * The pain had a specific cause, and it wasn't sin.
>
> * The pain didn't go away for years, even though I prayed and begged God to help me.
>
> * Until I dealt with the cause, the distress could not be alleviated, no matter how much I prayed.
>
> * I intuited the cause a long time before I was willing to deal with it.
>
> * Once I was free, the only reason I *stayed* free was that the pain was so great that I strongly desired and fought for freedom.

Many people find they need to reach a point of significant pain before they are willing to abandon things that are making them ill. How fortunate are the people who don't need pain to force them to choose habits that are healthy!

Complete victory is possible for you

Perhaps the primary lesson I learned from my experience with caffeine is the level of complete victory that is possible for us.

Caffeine was woven into every part of my life. I did *not* want to give it up. Even after I discovered that it caused my headaches,

I tried to hang on to "just a little bit" of it. Initially, it was an ongoing battle to remind myself that I was *not* going to give in to my desires for it. After time went by, the difficulty of that battle diminished. Now I don't face it at all. I can be in the presence of coffee and chocolate and cola and not desire them. They are not for me.

This tells me that in other areas of my life, where I am not yet so completely free, I can be. Complete freedom is possible. We can each choose things that bring health, even if we are strongly addicted to unhealthy patterns. Over time, as we continue to resist, the temptation to do harmful things decreases. Eventually we can be free even of the temptation itself. The temptation will no longer have power; it won't seem appealing.

You can have that kind of complete victory. It may take time, but it is possible for us all.

You can choose a healthy reality

In Anthony Robbins' best-seller *Awaken the Giant Within*, he gives a step-by-step strategy for achieving freedom. He writes:

> If you and I want to change our behavior, there is only one effective way to do it: we must link unbearable and immediate sensations of pain to our old behavior, and incredible and immediate sensations of pleasure to a new one.[10]

This is effectively what I did – although at the time I hadn't heard of Tony or the research on which he reports.

Tony says freedom is possible for you in any area of your life, even areas where you have repeatedly failed in the past. The five steps that Tony recommends:

1) Identify what you want. Be very clear and specific. Deeply feel what this change would mean to you.

2) Link intense pain to not changing, and intense pleasure to immediate change. Tony writes:

> If we gather a set of strong enough reasons to change, we can change in a *minute* something we've failed to change for years.[11] . . . If you've tried many times to make a change and you've failed to do so, this simply means that the level of pain for failing to change is not intense enough. . . . Ask yourself pain-inducing questions: "What will this cost me if I *don't* change?"[12]

Tony correctly notes that we often let the cost of change keep us from changing. We forget to compare that cost to the cost of *not* changing.

3) Interrupt the habit *when it is occurring.* Take some jarring action that will break the spell. For instance, you could have a glass of water out, ready to throw on yourself. When you lapse into the habit you want to change, dump the water on your head. A couple times of cleaning up will probably be enough to break the pattern. Whatever jarring action you choose, the trick is to interrupt your habit *when it is in process.*

4) Replace the habit with something else that gives great satisfaction. This can be any healthy activity that is rewarding to you.

I have found the greatest gains often come from doing something I know to be good that I have been afraid to do in the past. One friend says he gets the greatest help from activities that draw him closer to God – e.g., doing good deeds with others, prayer and studying the Bible. Try several of these and find out what is the most rewarding for you.

5) Make the replacement activity in step four a new habit.

Many people who make a good start but fall back to their old behavior haven't followed through on steps four and five. The old behavior is there for a reason; it provided some benefit.

Actively replace it with something healthier that will provide a similar benefit.

By intentionally following these five steps, you can break any pattern and adopt a new one that is better for you.

Get started now!

Tony's strategy will work for any unhealthy behavior in any area of your life. This represents a lot of territory for us, and we should get started now!

Some people will object that their main problem is a *symptom* (e.g., cancer), and since they don't know what caused it, they don't know what behaviors to change. For many of us, however, we have some good guesses of what kinds of behaviors we need (and want!) to change, even if we lack certainty. It's worth it to work on those guesses. (And if you don't have any guesses, ask people who are healthy what they think. In many cases, the cause is probably known.)

If you truly have no guesses even after asking healthy people what they think, pick the first area of your life that comes to mind and get practice changing your behavior in that area. Your life will improve, even if your main problem is not addressed. And by getting practice with the technique, you will be ready to apply it to your main problem when you intuit the cause.

While you are working on side issues, you can ask God to provide insight into what is causing your symptoms. If you're taking in poison, you may have to change your behavior before you get the healing you desire. Poisons include doubt, disbelief, gossip, envy, cruelty, bitterness, unforgiveness, slander, jealousy, adultery and the like as well as things like carcinogens and foods you are allergic to.

Ask God for the key to your breakthrough

In stuck cases, where you haven't yet discovered the key that will unlock your healing, it can be helpful to cry out to God, asking for ideas of what you need to do. Even the world's most famous healing professionals get sick and experience pain; even they benefit from this kind of prayer.

By coincidence one day, two Christian television programs that emphasize God's power to heal devoted their entire broadcasts to discussions of incidents where the pastors themselves were unable to experience healing, in spite of their own best efforts. On the programs, four of the most noted healers of our day talked about their own long periods of pain.

One of them, Jerry Savelle, talked about how he had constant pain in his neck and shoulders. He said he would go to a meeting where he would pray for others to receive healing and the pain in his own neck would be so great he could hardly turn his head. Someone would have to massage his shoulders to give him enough relief to go on with the program.

At the meetings, Jerry would preach and encourage people, but when he got back to his hotel room he couldn't sleep because of the pain. "This went on for years and years," he said, "and I *know* how to believe God for healing." One day, flying back from some meetings, the pain was extra intense. Jerry had his daughter massage his shoulders while he sat with a cup of coffee. Agonized by the pain, he said out loud, "Lord, I'm not a novice. I know how to believe you for healing. I know [the reason I'm not healed] is not you; I know it's not your word. What am I doing wrong?"

Jerry says he sensed a one-word response: "Caffeine." The answer surprised Jerry – he was expecting something much different – but the pain in his neck was so bad he was willing to try anything.

It's worth it to find the solution

Things didn't get immediately better. Jerry says, "For the next five days, I had caffeine withdrawals, and I thought my head was going to split. I'm telling you it was the worst five days I've ever spent in my life." But on the sixth day, he was free of pain and he slept through the night without waking. For eight years his neck and shoulder pain have been gone.

This is not a book about caffeine, so I wish my headaches and Jerry's neck trouble were caused by different things. But, by coincidence, they had the same cause. I include Jerry's story because I think it illustrates a number of helpful things.

1) Even the pros get caught in situations that seem unbearable and unsolvable. If you haven't had relief yet, you're not alone.

2) Jerry knew all about the power of healing prayer, and many people had prayed for him, but that hadn't helped his particular condition. Jerry had to make a change before he could be freed of his neck pain.

3) Jerry had been drinking coffee since he was 12. As a result, he never suspected the source of his trouble – and might never have discovered it if he hadn't cried out and asked God to identify it. Many people in stuck conditions might benefit from repeating Jerry's prayer:

> God, I know the problem is not with you or your promises. I must be doing something that prevents me from being healed. Please show me what it is. Thank you.

Then stay open to the faint impressions you have.

Don't expect a bolt of lightning. Ask yourself: "What impressions have I been ignoring? What ideas have I discarded because I thought, 'That couldn't be it.'?" If you have an impression that defies logic, it is worth exploring. Logic is accurate only when all the facts are known, and in this case, you don't consciously know all the facts.

4) The pathway to healing sometimes involves greater suffering. To get to the freedom of day six, Jerry had to endure

the withdrawal pains of days one through five.

You *can* be healed

There *is* a solution to your healing. It may be that you need to meet someone who has more knowledge or skill. It may be that you have to wait through a process. It may be that you need to make a change. It may be that a procedure needs to be discovered or invented. But there *is* a solution, and it is worth pursuing. Be like the woman Jesus mentioned who kept demanding what she needed until she got it.[13]

Unfortunately for some people, they never discover what will help during the course of their lifetimes. The next chapter discusses the hope that is waiting for people in those situations. But don't give up early! Keep seeking a solution until your days end. Many people have recovered after everyone else had given up hope, including their doctors.

Checklist

_____ Ask God for the key to your breakthrough. Listen to sensations in your body, intuitions in your mind, and pictures in your imagination. What do they suggest?

_____ Ask yourself, "Why do I need this illness?"

_____ Ask yourself, "What was happening before I got sick?"

_____ Ask yourself, "Is this disease symbolic of anything in my life?"

_____ Ask yourself, "What do I need to change to become healthy?"

_____ Identify any natural laws you know you are breaking. Start following them as an experiment to see what will happen.

_____ What are your ten favorite foods? Do you note any patterns? (Sugar, salt, alcohol, fat, a recurring ingredient, etc.) Try eliminating foods belonging to one of the patterns you see for a month. What happens?

_____ Follow Tony Robbins' plan:

Identify what you want. Be specific.

Link intense pain to not changing and intense pleasure to changing.

Interrupt the old habit while it is occurring.

Replace the habit with something that gives satisfaction.

_____ Don't give up.

Questions for Discussion

1) What are some long-standing problems that you face?

2) What changes would help resolve them? (Make a list of ideas that occur to you, even if you don't have a lot of confidence that they'll work.)

3) Have you tried making these changes? If not, why not? If so, what happened?

4) Pick a current health condition and spend some time with the question, "Why do you need this illness?" What kinds of things occur to you?

5) What behaviors do you engage in that you know are not healthy? What benefits do you receive from these behaviors?

6) What conditions do you have where the root cause is unknown to you? Ask God to identify the key to your breakthrough. What intuitions come to you?

7) What is one area of your life that you want to change? Be very clear and specific about what you want. Allow your emotions about what this change would mean to you to surface. What feelings do you have?

8) What would it feel like if you changed today? What would it feel like if you never changed?

9) What is one way you will interrupt what you want to change when it is occurring?

10) What will you replace the habit with?

11) What else in this chapter caught your attention?

Chapter 8

You Can Be Healed At The End

Many times people are healed with just one prayer. Sometimes people are healed through the process of time. Often people are healed after they make a change. But sometimes people do not find healing in this lifetime. The Bible promises that these friends will not be forgotten. John, a follower of Jesus, saw a vision about the end of time. He wrote:

> I saw a new heaven and a new earth; for the first heaven and the first earth had passed away, and the sea was no more. And I saw the holy city, the new Jerusalem, coming down out of heaven from God, prepared as a bride adorned for her husband. And I heard a loud voice from the throne saying, "See, the home of God is among mortals. He will dwell with them as their God; they will be his peoples, and God himself will be with them; he will wipe every tear from their eyes. Death will be no more; mourning and crying and pain will be no more, for the first things have passed away." [1]

People who experience tremendous pain in this life have this promise that God not only sees their suffering, but God is planning to wipe every tear from their eyes and to remove their pain in the life after death.

Express your feelings to God who loves you

People who are suffering sometimes find comfort in the Psalms, the songbook of the Bible. Psalm 23 is one that many people turn to. It says:

> The LORD is my shepherd; I shall not want.
> He makes me to lie down in green pastures;

He leads me beside the still waters. He restores my soul.
He leads me in the paths of righteousness
for his name's sake.
Even though I walk through the valley of the shadow of
death, I will fear no evil, for you are with me.
Your rod and your staff comfort me.
You prepare a table before me in the presence of my
enemies; You anoint my head with oil. My cup runs over.
Surely goodness and mercy will follow me all the days
of my life, and I will dwell in the house of the LORD
forever.[2]

Some of the psalms in the Bible express anger, discontent, sadness and frustration. Others express confidence, joy and peace in spite of appearances. No matter what your mood, you will find that people in the Bible have expressed something similar in the past. Since that is the case, feel free to honestly tell God what you are experiencing. Write your own psalms that describe what you are feeling.

Pray for researchers working on your condition

If you have a condition that is currently beyond our medical and spiritual expertise, continue to receive medical aid and prayer for healing from experts. But while you are receiving prayer for yourself, be sure to pray for other people in your condition and for researchers investigating cures to your problem. The solutions researchers find may be in time to help you. Even if they are not, they will certainly be in time to help generations of people after you, and you know by direct experience what a blessing that will be.

In 1916, a polio epidemic killed 6,000 people in the United States and paralyzed 27,000 more. Many survivors were unable to walk without the use of braces. Others had to stay in respirators called Iron Lungs, gasping for air. There was nothing parents could do: children died and were crippled overnight. But the anguished cries of all those parents led to medical discoveries that saved the lives of generations that came after.

In the early 1950's polio was still impacting more than 20,000 lives each year, but in 1955 polio vaccination began. Five years later, the number of cases had dropped 85%. By 1979 there were only ten cases of polio in the United States. By 2005, no wild polio had been reported for more than 20 years. Although polio still persists in other parts of the world, in the United States it has been eliminated. (1,604 cases of polio were reported in 2009, primarily in India, Nigeria, Pakistan, Chad, Sudan and Guinea.)

It may be that you are at a point in history before an invention is discovered that will cure your condition. If that is the case, your prayers and the prayers of your friends and family can move us closer to a cure.

Or it may be that you are at a point in history where the cure is known and available – but in a different part of the world than the area where you live. If that is the case, it is worth pursuing health for you and the other people in your country.

God bless you as you pray and intercede for yourself and the world. Let your prayers be the turning point for others in your condition.

Some people are "healed perfectly"

Cleo contracted infectious hepatitis when she was 49. Many people prayed for her, but after only three weeks, she died. Her daughter writes:

> This caused much confusion and bewilderment among the members of our congregation because everyone prayed believing she would recover. A comment by the adult Bible study teacher was most helpful to me. His remark: "When we prayed for healing, we had no idea Cleo would be healed perfectly."

Sometimes when we pray for someone and they die, there

is a sense of failure of those who have been praying. I believe it might be because of the way we think about death – so often thinking of it as an undesired end, rather than looking at it as a process and being "perfectly healed" and going home.

The daughter writes that following this incident she felt comforted by Isaiah 55:8-9:

> For my thoughts are not your thoughts, nor are your ways my ways, says the LORD. For as the heavens are higher than the earth, so are my ways higher than your ways and my thoughts than your thoughts.

Knowing that God who loved her might have a different way of looking at her mother's situation helped her through her time of grief.

Be prepared

Be prepared for the end. Death may not come for decades, but you want to have a will or a living trust in place. You want to have forgiven everyone. You want to have told your friends and family that you love them. Be ready for the end, whenever it comes.

Don't give up until it's over

One of the people impacted by polio was Franklin Delano Roosevelt. He got the disease at age 39 and had to use a wheelchair for the rest of his life. But that didn't stop him from becoming a beloved President of the United States. Some diseases will cause major debilitating changes – but as long as you have breath, you are able to create beauty and joy for others. Even bedridden people can write poetry, pray for the nations, and enhance the lives of others. You may not feel like it, but it's worth it, nonetheless. Let your life be a blessing to others.

Checklist

_____ Accept God's mercy (which flows even when you are in pain).

_____ Read the Psalms to see if they provide encouragement. If not, write your own songs to God that capture *your* feelings.

_____ Speak honestly to God about how you feel.

_____ Pray for others in your condition around the world.

_____ Pray for researchers working on your condition.

_____ Make sure your will or living trust is complete.

_____ Forgive everyone.

_____ Tell your friends and family that you love them.

_____ Don't give up until it's over.

_____ Let your life be a blessing to others.

Questions for Discussion

1)   Who do you know that has endured years of suffering?

2)   How do you treat them?

3)   What long-term conditions capture your heart?

4)   What could you do to help people with these conditions?

5)   How do you feel when you hear that God will wipe every
     tear from people's eyes, that eventually mourning and crying
     and pain will be no more?

6)   What researchers are you praying for?

7)   What do you think about the concept of people being
     "perfectly healed"?

8)   Do you have a will or living trust? If not, when will you
     complete one?

9)   Who have you not forgiven? When will you forgive them?

10) Who have you not told that you love them? When will you
     tell them?

11) What could you do to let your life be a blessing to others?
     When will you do it?

12) What else in this chapter caught your attention?

Section C

Ideas For People
Who Are Praying For Others

Chapter 9

How To Increase
Your Effectiveness In Prayer

If I wanted to move a bucketful of dirt from the front yard of a house to the back yard, it wouldn't take much effort. I'd be able to do it even if I were in poor condition, even if I were not very motivated, even if I didn't have much time, even if I didn't have a shovel. It's a small job, requiring very little ability and resources.

On the other hand, if I decided to buy Mt. Rushmore and move it intact to my property, things would be different. The legal wrangling over such an operation – to take a national treasure and move it to a private yard – would be so intense that most people would say the job could never be done. Even if I got permission, the problems associated with the task itself might seem insurmountable. Moving all that rock such a long distance would require tremendous time, effort, coordination, energy and money. But to move it intact? And undamaged? Impossible.

Well, of course it's not impossible. Anything is possible. But this particular operation would be so expensive and so fraught with risk and so difficult that it would require tremendous resources – some not invented yet – to pull it off.

When people pray, they ask for things that vary between the equivalent of moving a small amount of dirt a few feet to moving Mt. Rushmore. Some requests don't take much effort to fulfill. Others are quite a bit harder. Nothing is impossible for God,[1] but often people and their beliefs limit what God can do.[2]

You can become more effective in prayer

Sometimes people are surprised by the concept that they can

become more effective in prayer. They understand that a gardener can improve by learning more effective planting techniques. They understand that a business manager can improve through coaching and practice. They may even understand that a preacher can get better through practice and various disciplines. But somehow they put prayer in a separate category. It's not! You can get better at prayer, just like you can get better at anything else. This chapter describes a few things that will help you become more effective when you pray.

A number of helpful ideas that were mentioned in previous chapters will only be summarized here:

1) Ask God if a change is needed before healing can come for a specific individual. Does the person need to give up certain foods or behaviors or ways of thinking?

2) Ask God if a change *in you* will help you be more effective.

3) Keep track of progress, no matter how small, and thank God for it. When a situation is stuck, even a small change is worth celebrating. Rejoicing over small changes will pave the way for more changes down the road.

4) Use your imagination to let your subconscious know what you want. Picture yourself successfully healing others through prayer.

5) Ask people in stuck conditions, "Why do you need this illness?" The question will help people discover things they need to change before they can become well.

6) Ask, "What was happening before you got sick?" This question will help people make connections between their illnesses and what led to them.

This chapter will focus on eight remaining ideas:

7) Act on Jesus' authority. Ask for things as if you were Jesus.

8) Align yourself with God's ways.

9) Ask God for a greater ability to heal people.

10) Regularly pray for others.

11) Fast and ask to become more effective.

12) Ask for greater faith.

13) Focus on what you want.

14) Be steadfast.

You become more effective
when you obey Jesus' command to heal the sick

7) Act on Jesus' authority. Ask for things as if you were Jesus.

We gain effectiveness when we are acting under the authority of a person or entity more powerful than ourselves. Imagine Jane, a flight attendant for an airline. She is somewhat shy. She weighs 110 pounds. On her own, she's not very powerful. But when she gets on an airplane in her vocation as flight attendant, you better do what she says. Interfering with her performance is a felony. Of course, when she walks off the plane, she gives up that authority until her next flight. The authority she has aboard a plane is something that is loaned to her for a particular assignment.

Someone who is executor of an estate has a similar kind of authority. The person's own bank account may be quite empty. But as executor of the estate, that person's signature might carry considerable weight. The power of the estate is loaned to the person for that particular assignment.

That's how it is when we obey Jesus' command to heal others. We may feel – and be – inadequate. But we are not acting on our own authority when we pray for healing. We are acting on Jesus'

112 How To Increase Your Effectiveness In Prayer

command to heal the sick. We have his power at our disposal when we do what he says.[3] You don't have to worry about your own ability as you pray for people for healing; the power to heal doesn't come from you. It flows through you from God.

Ask and keep asking

Sometimes people think there is a limit to what they can receive from God. They try to limit their requests to what is "sensible." They would never ask for anything big. Others who think there is a limit to God's mercy don't want to ask for anything small. They don't want to "use up" all their requests before they come to something they *really* need. Neither view of God is biblical.

The Bible says that God is waiting to give us good things, but we haven't asked.[4] The biblical view is not that God has limited love for us, but that God *is* love. There is no limit to God's mercy or favor for us because it never ends. People can ask for *anything.* Jesus refers to God as Father in John 16:23-24 and says:

> If you ask anything of the Father in my name, he will give it to you. Until now you have not asked for anything in my name. Ask and you will receive, so that your joy may be complete.

Anything! That's a great promise! It would be worth it for us to discover what it meant to ask God "in Jesus name." Does it mean we can ask for something, add the words "in Jesus' name" at the end and then get what we want? Are these words a magic formula, an incantation like "abracadabra" that works?

Most people would guess that probably wasn't what Jesus meant. So what do his words mean?

Ask for things Jesus would ask for

Many Bible verses talk about doing things "in someone's

name" or "in God's name." If you study those verses, you will see that the phrase has several different meanings.[5] The meaning that fits best with Jesus' statement in John 16 is doing something in the place of another. It has the connotation of being an ambassador standing in for a nation. Doing something "in Jesus' name" means doing something on behalf of Jesus, as if you were him. Given that understanding, the sense of the verse would be:

> If you ask anything of the Father as if you were me, he will give it to you. Until now you have not asked for anything as if you were me. Ask and you will receive, so that your joy may be complete.

This is an exciting way to look at the verse! It encourages us to engage our imaginations to ask, "What would Jesus do if he were here?" and then to stand in for him, asking God for what Jesus himself would have asked. If you have this understanding, using the words "in Jesus' name" in your prayers can be a helpful reminder of what you are doing.

We gain effectiveness when we align ourselves with God's ways

8) Align yourself with God's ways.

Because the power to heal flows from God, we gain effectiveness when we align our lives with God's purposes. The more we are in line with God's intent, the more effective we will be. That's one of the reasons it is so helpful to read the Bible. It lets you know how the universe works, and what God's intent is. For example, 1 Timothy 2:4 says:

> God our Savior. . . desires everyone to be saved and to come to the knowledge of the truth.

This verse lets us know that people are never so far gone that God doesn't yearn for their rescue. God wants *everyone* to be rescued. We can claim that promise when we are praying for someone who needs to be saved from trouble – especially if it is someone everyone else has given up on.

The Bible is filled with verses like this. The more you know, the closer you can model your life on God's intention, and the more authority you will have.[6]

Ask God for the gift of healing

9) Ask God for greater ability to heal people.

Some people have natural talents for various tasks. National Basketball Association professionals, for instance, are great at basketball. *Anyone* can play the game. Even me. But it's more fun to watch an NBA pro than to watch me play. The NBA pros are gifted.

If you aren't gifted in healing, you can still pray for people and see them recover. But if you have the gift of healing, you will be more effective in your prayers. Similarly, if you don't have the gift, your effectiveness will increase if you bring along someone who does. It's like playing a game of city league basketball with an NBA pro on your team. *You* haven't gotten any better. But your team's effectiveness will skyrocket.

Paul, an early follower of Jesus, wrote that God's Spirit gives each person at least one gift to be used for the common good. One of the gifts he mentions is the gift of healing and another is the gift of miracles.[7]

Paul wrote that people should strive for the more important gifts.[8] If you'd like the gift of healing or of miracles, ask God. But don't stop there. Striving for something means actively pursuing it. Get training from ministry teams that have the gift. Have someone with the gift place their hands on you and pray that you receive the gift. Even better, you could volunteer to be their apprentice so you could learn from them firsthand. Many great leaders were apprenticed by other leaders.

Get some practice

10) Regularly pray for others.

One of the reasons NBA stars are fun to watch, besides their natural gifting, is that they practice. Everyone gets better with practice, even people with a natural talent for something. I know that from my experience in painting. I am very good at abstract art.[9] But if I haven't painted in a couple weeks, it takes time for me to get good again. Being just a couple days out of practice makes a noticeable difference. The only way to stay at your best is to stay in practice, even if you are gifted.

The more you practice praying for people for healing, the better you will become. Failures will drive you to learn more. Experience will teach you patterns and techniques that are helpful. Victories will encourage you to try even greater things. Ongoing practice is one of the most valuable things you can do. Malcolm Gladwell reports that mastery of a field comes after about 10,000 hours of practice.[10] It's time to get started!

Fast and pray

11) Fast and ask to become more effective.

Jesus once told his followers that the reason they had no success in a particular situation was that they hadn't fasted and prayed beforehand.[11] Before you get into a situation where you need to be stronger, you can fast and ask God for power, for ability, for training, for insight, for the right team of helpers, and for anything else you need.

There are many different kinds of fasts. One of the most common is where people give up one or more kinds of food or drink. Jesus fasted this way at least once – for 40 days – and he expected his followers to fast from food once he died.[12]

When Jesus taught his disciples about fasting, however, he didn't teach them practical details of what to give up and for how long. Instead, he taught about the more important aspect of a person's heart. Jesus was concerned that fasting would become a source of pride, and he told a story about a man whose prayers went unheard because he was so proud – even though he regularly fasted.[13] The prophet Zechariah described a case where God rejected *70 years* worth of fasting![14] That's not the position we want to be in!

Jesus cautioned his disciples not to call attention to their fasting by looking unhappy:

> Whenever you fast, do not look dismal, like the hypocrites, for they disfigure their faces so as to show others that they are fasting. Truly I tell you, they have received their reward. But when you fast, put oil on your head and wash your face, so that your fasting may be seen not by others but by your Father who is in secret; and your Father who sees in secret will reward you.[15]

One of the best fasts is to bring about justice

Even though fasting from food gets most of our attention, it is not the only – or even the preferred – fast discussed in the Bible. In one of the most important passages in the Bible on fasting, Isaiah says that God prefers fasts that bring about justice and mercy. Isaiah 58:6-9a says:

> Is not this the fast that I choose:
> to loose the bonds of injustice,
> to undo the thongs of the yoke,
> to let the oppressed go free, and to break every yoke?
> Is it not to share your bread with the hungry,
> and bring the homeless poor into your house;
> when you see the naked, to cover them,
> and not to hide yourself from your own kin?

Isaiah shows that many kinds of actions count as fasting, and that God especially favors fasts that help the poor. You might consider what kind of fast would be appropriate for the condition you are praying about.

We become more effective
when others believe God will act

12) Ask for greater faith for yourself and others.

Surprisingly, our effectiveness is impacted not only by our own faith, but by the level of faith of the people around us. When Jesus was in his hometown, the Bible says he was unable to do deeds of power there because the people around him lacked confidence in his ability.[16] Jesus' own faith hadn't changed; what hampered his ability to do miracles was the deep doubt of others.

As mentioned in chapter three, if we're surrounded by doubting people, we'll have better results if we help them to develop faith or if we move away from them before praying. This is what Jesus did when he had to pray for an especially hard case, a child who had died. He cleared out all the people who were laughing at him and allowed only the child's immediate family and his closest followers to stay.

Ask believing

Jesus says, "Whatever you ask for in prayer, believe that you have received it, and it will be yours."[17] Notice that Jesus says "*believe* that you have received it," not "*beg* that you have received it." Believe. And also notice that Jesus says to believe "that you *have* received it," not "that you *will* receive it." Many people testify that when they began acting as if something were already true, they walked into the place where it *was* true.

Dr. Maxwell Maltz, a cosmetic surgeon, once saw a 20-year-old man become old almost overnight. A girlfriend had told the young man that she could not marry him because his lower lip was too big. The young man wanted Dr. Maltz to correct the size of his lip, anticipating a speedy marriage would result.

Dr. Maltz guessed otherwise. He reduced the size of the

man's lip for a modest fee on the condition that the man tell his girlfriend he had spent everything he had on the operation to give her what she wanted. Maltz suspected she was not being truthful.

As it turned out, Maltz was right. When the boyfriend displayed his new lip and announced it had cost him everything to please her, she said she had never loved him and had only been interested in his money. That would have been devastating enough, but then she went further and placed a Voodoo curse on him. Both were from an island in the West Indies where people believe in such curses.

Soon afterwards, the young man noticed a bump on the inside of his lip. Someone who knew about the curse diagnosed it as an "African Bug" that would deplete all his strength and vitality. He quit eating and sleeping. By the time Maltz saw him, the young man – who had been very athletic – appeared to have aged by decades. His hands shook; his cheeks were sunken; he had lost about 30 pounds. Maltz writes:

> After a quick examination of his mouth, I assured [him] I could get rid of the African Bug in less than 30 minutes, which I did. The bump which had caused all the trouble was merely a small bit of scar tissue from his operation. I removed it, held it in my hand, and showed it to him. The important thing is he saw the truth and believed it.

A month or two later, Maltz received a picture of the young man, fully recovered in appearance. Maltz writes he "had grown young again – overnight."[18]

The young man had quickly aged because he acted differently when he believed he was cursed. His belief led him to quit eating and sleeping, which caused conditions that reinforced his belief. When he believed he was cured, he acted differently (he started eating, sleeping and exercising) and quickly recovered.

Faith is a very important factor, partly because it impacts your actions. In fact, faith is so important that it sometimes matters less what you believe *in* (e.g., a curse or a placebo) than it matters *what* you believe (e.g., that you'll get well or that you'll get sick). Neither the girlfriend's curse nor placebos have any power on their own. What makes them effective is the *belief* that they have power. Faith, by itself, is so powerful that it is effective *all on its own*, regardless of what a person has faith *in*. Of course, if you have faith in something real, you're miles ahead.

Jesus taught on the importance of faith on a regular basis.[19] Fortunately, greater faith is something you can ask for.[20]

Focus on what you want

13) Focus on what you want.

Pastor John Kilpatrick of Pensacola, Florida, had wanted an orchestra for his church for years – so when his church built a new worship center, they included space for an orchestra pit. John writes he would go to the area on Saturdays and pray:

> God . . . You know I've never had an orchestra in my church. . . . I need an orchestra. When are You going to give me one? When is our church going to have the wonderful sound of brass instruments You helped. . . create?[21]

John says he prayed like that for a long time. But one day John felt like God interrupted him and asked, "Instead of speaking curses, whining, and complaining about your desire for an orchestra, why don't you bless it?" John says:

> I was stunned. But as I pondered the content of my praying, I realized God was right. I had been using prayer to complain to God – in effect, "cursing" the situation.

> By next Saturday evening, my prayers for an orchestra changed dramatically. Standing in the sunken area, I began anew. "Father, I bless this area. I thank You that one day a

tremendous orchestra will fill this space. I thank You that
Brownsville Assembly of God is attracting people with
new talent, including those who play brass instruments. I
bless this area in Your Name, Lord, and say that it is fertile
ground for an orchestra."[22]

Within three months, God brought a trumpet player to the
church, and the trumpeter became the start of the orchestra. John
says he had prayed for an orchestra for 19 years without results.
But three months after changing the way he prayed, he got the
start of what he had longed for all those years. When he changed
from complaining about the visible present to thanking God for
the preferred future, the future he wanted came about.

Like John, some of us may need to change how we're praying.

We are more effective when we do not waver

14) Be steadfast.

Sometimes people waver in their prayers. They want the
result but don't want to do what is required to bring it about.
So they go back and forth in their requests. They're like waves
at the shoreline – first crashing forward, then pulling back.
Even though they are in endless motion, they make no ultimate
progress. James says:

> Ask in faith, never doubting, for the one who doubts is like
> a wave of the sea, driven and tossed by the wind; for the
> doubter, being double-minded and unstable in every way,
> must not expect to receive anything from the Lord.[23]

Increase your effectiveness

The world is counting on your prayers, and God has already
promised to give you all you ask for that is good. If you haven't
gotten an answer for something that seems good, try increasing
your effectiveness by following the ideas mentioned in this
chapter.

Checklist

_____   Ask God if a change is needed before healing can come, either in the patient or in you.

_____   Keep track of progress, no matter how small, and thank God for it.

_____   Picture yourself successfully healing others.

_____   Ask people in stuck conditions, "Why do you need this illness?"

_____   Ask, "What was happening before you got sick?"

_____   Ask for things as if you were Jesus.

_____   Follow God's advice on how to live.

_____   Ask God for the gift of healing.

_____   Blend prayer with action.

_____   Bring along people with the gift of healing.

_____   Practice.

_____   Fast and pray in advance for ability, training, insight, the right team of helpers, and anything else you need.

_____   Help people who are poor (it's one form of fasting).

_____   Pray near people of faith and away from doubters.

_____   Focus on the positive outcome you desire and thank God for it. Believe you can receive it.

_____   Maintain one course. Don't waver.

Questions for Discussion

1) What prayers have you had answered?

2) To what extent is your life aligned with what God says is the best way to live?

3) Do you have the gift of healing? (If not, have you asked for it and pursued it?)

4) Who do you know who has the gift of healing?

5) How much practice do you get each day, praying for people?

6) What kinds of fasts do you practice?

7) When you pray for others, how sensitive are you to the presence of scoffers in the area?

8) What is the level of your own faith for healing?

9) For what kinds of requests do you seem to usually get positive answers?

10) What have you been praying for like Pastor John Kilpatrick was initially, focusing on the undesired present rather than the hoped for future?

11) What experiences have you had or heard about where faith made a difference in an outcome?

12) In what areas in your life do you waver, not staying focused on one direction?

13) What else in this chapter caught your attention?

Chapter 10

Healing For Cases
With No Physical Cause

Many illnesses have a physical cause. Some do not. For some conditions, the causes are mental, emotional, or spiritual.

Ideas can cause diseases

Suppose Robert thinks, "People who do what I did should be punished." If he becomes sick and you help him recover, you will have helped. But if he keeps the belief that he should be punished, his subconscious will continue to look for ways to draw punishment into his life. For complete healing, he needs to change his thinking and accept God's forgiveness.

Luckily, we don't have to worry about every idea we've ever had. The thoughts that impact health are the vows and statements we make with strong emotional force or the ideas we entertain regularly, not the random thoughts that come to us throughout the day.

For example, if Sarah says, "I'm *never* getting hurt like that again," and sticks with that idea, it may come to limit her in ways she did not intend. She may miss the greatest opportunities of her life in an attempt to reduce pain.

At this point, it might be helpful for you to make a list of vows you have made over the course of your life. Ask God to help bring them to mind. When you look at your list, check to see if the vows are still in your best interest. Some vows you made in the past are probably no longer helpful.

If you have some you want to change, you can change them. Use the same level of emotional energy as when you made the vow in the first place. Actively imagine the pain of keeping the vow. Then actively imagine the positive consequences of your new thought. You may need to repeat this process a few times. But you can replace an old standard of behavior with a new one. (For more discussion of this process, see the description of how to replace a habit on page 93. If you're still having trouble, see the helpful book *Change Anything* by Kerry Patterson, et al.[1])

Some diseases have spiritual causes

About the time of the Civil War, many Americans did not believe in germs. Some people had never heard of them. Other people only believed in things they could see, and since they couldn't see anything on their hands, they didn't believe germs were on their hands.

When microscopes allowed people to get a close-up view, they changed their minds. Suddenly they could see things that were invisible to the naked eye. Consciousness of germs helped people adopt better sanitation. They washed their hands more frequently and reduced their contact with waste. As a result, the health of soldiers and of the general public began to improve.

When people were ignorant of germs, the germs had far more power. Once people knew germs existed, they began taking sensible precautions.

In Jesus' day, there was a debate similar to the Civil War conversation about whether germs existed or not. In Jesus' day, the topic was whether evil spirits existed. (Evil spirits are also called demons.) Like germs, evil spirits couldn't be seen, so their existence couldn't be proved. Many religious leaders denied their existence,[2] but Jesus taught that evil spirits exist and demonstrated that they harm people's health. [3]

For a good part of my life, I thought I knew better than Jesus. I figured if Jesus had been alive in the 21st century, he would have used different words to describe the conditions he was seeing. You might suppose I could have seen the irony of thinking "Jesus is the Son of God" and "I know better than Jesus." But I didn't figure that out. What changed my mind was an experience. I finally saw someone afflicted by a demon who was set free.

You may be skeptical, as I once was. I can certainly understand. All I can say is, the person that I saw set free is very, very glad that someone knew how to deal with the problem.

Sometimes people think they are being "rational" by rejecting the existence of spirits, since spirits are invisible. This is not a very scientific approach. Scientists believe in lots of things that cannot be seen, from very tiny particles to very large stellar objects. But if you don't believe in spirits, you are not alone. All I ask is that you keep an open mind and look at what Jesus did and taught on the subject.

Jesus set people free

Jesus routinely set people free from the influence of demons as part of his ministry.[4] In addition, he expected his followers to cast out demons[5] and they did.[6] In many of the reports of these encounters, we have no details except that the people were healed. Other times we hear that the demons recognized Jesus' authority, yelling that he was the Son of God[7] or shrieking before leaving.[8]

In some cases, however, we have more details about their activity. These accounts are curious. Many people today think demons cause lust, anger, or sinful thoughts. They might. But the records of Jesus do not talk not about these kinds of things. Instead, they mention the illnesses the demons were causing.

Demons that Jesus dealt with caused people to appear to be:
* mute[9]
* bent over with osteoporosis[10]
* epileptic[11]
* antisocial and self-mutilating[12]

 * tormented[13]
 * suicidal[14]

I don't suppose that is a complete list of illnesses demons mimic; it is a list of the diseases mentioned in the records we have about Jesus.

The next point is very important: Diseases can be caused by many different things. People can become mute because of conditions in pregnancy, or viruses, or genetic disorders, or traumatic events, or ideas and vows, or environmental poisons, or dozens of other possibilities. If you see someone who is mute, you should not assume that a demon is behind it. But neither should you eliminate any of the possible reasons for a condition just because you find them distasteful. Some percentage of the people who appear mute are not; they have a demon that is causing the person to be unable to speak. These people won't respond to medical treatment because they don't have a medical problem. If the spirit leaves, they will be able to talk.

Unfortunately, many Christians and churches avoid this topic. There are lots of reasons for this. One is a lack of faith in what Jesus taught on this subject. Another is that many of us want to avoid messy encounters. We value relative quiet over the possibility of freedom for demonized people. If a demon is going to shriek when it leaves, we'd rather the person stay tormented. If you sit with the reality of that last statement for a while, you'll come to realize how much we need to repent of attitudes that keep people trapped in lifelong illnesses.

Tell demons to leave

Casting out demons is fairly straightforward. Jesus gave his followers authority over demons. If you are a follower of Jesus, accept that authority, and tell the demon to leave. It's that simple. If you'll try it, you'll likely find yourself as surprised as the original disciples, who reported their successes to Jesus with amazement.[15]

Those disciples found that some spirits are easier to get rid of than others. They had quite a bit of success initially. Then they encountered a demon they couldn't get rid of. Jesus successfully got rid of the demon for them, then told his followers they needed to pray in advance for the power to defeat demons like that one. Some versions of the text add that fasting is also important in such cases.[16]

Take Jesus' advice and ask now for the ability to meet challenges you will encounter in the future.

You don't have to be directly involved

I was on an airplane once where the baby behind me started wailing the moment the plane was airborne. I'm sympathetic; as a youth I boarded a plane with an ear infection and found out how extremely painful an airplane ride can be. As a result, on this flight I put up with the baby's crying for more than an hour while the parents tried everything they could to calm their child. The baby was in the seat directly behind me, so I got the wailing full blast.

Finally I was so irritated that I started to think about the problem. And at that point I realized the baby might not have a physical condition. What if a spirit was tormenting the baby? Silently I commanded, "Spirit tormenting that baby, be gone in Jesus name." The baby instantly quit crying and slept for the rest of the flight. I wished I had thought of it earlier. So did the parents and a lot of other relieved passengers, who never knew what happened.

Some people will think that the timing of my prayer and the baby's immediate peaceful state was a coincidence. They are welcome to their opinion. My opinion is that they aren't very good at math. The probability of such a coincidence is next to zero, given the thousands of seconds the baby could have quit crying before my prayer, and the thousands of seconds after my prayer that the crying could have resumed.

If you're willing to assume with me that it was not a coincidence that the baby quit crying, there are a couple lessons to learn. First, I didn't touch the baby. I didn't turn around to face the baby or the parents. They didn't even know I'd prayed. I just issued the command, silently.

I'm not saying that's how you should always do it. In many cases, it will be helpful to be with the person, look into their eyes, and speak words they can hear. Jesus modeled direct contact most of the time. But Jesus also healed people from a distance. The next time you see someone not responding to normal treatment, tell the spirit to go and see what happens. You can do this even if you're not in the same city.

Ask for spiritual discernment

If you want to get into this ministry on a regular basis, ask God for the ability to sense what's happening in the spiritual realm. It's not always as obvious as you might think. Many times religious people see what God is doing and reject it.[17] Other times they embrace things that God is opposed to.[18] If you're not paying attention, you can be fooled by appearances. Ask God for the ability to correctly discern hidden things.

You can call in an expert

In the medical community, people often specialize. Your doctor may recognize a condition but refer you to a specialist who deals with such cases more regularly. You can refer, also. If you encounter someone whose condition is beyond your training or ability, give it your best shot. If nothing happens, send them to someone with more experience.

When Jesus' disciples couldn't heal a suicidal, epileptic boy, they didn't tell him to go home. They had him wait for Jesus. In the same way, you may encounter some conditions that require specialists. I regularly refer people to see others with more power or experience in particular conditions. You can, too.

The power comes from Jesus

The ability to cast out demons comes from one's relationship with Jesus. Demons respond to Jesus because they recognize his authority and acknowledge that he is the Son of God. Jesus gives his followers the ability to cast out demons, and the demons (sometimes grudgingly) recognize that chain of command.

People who try to get rid of demons without recognizing the authority of Jesus and without being under his command can sometimes cast demons out.[19] But sometimes, the demons recognize the lack of authority and rebel. In one example in the Bible, a demonized person attacked seven men and bested them.[20]

Sometimes people read this story and completely miss the point. They decide to not get involved because the work is "too dangerous." But the seven were attacked because they had no authority. If you're a follower of Jesus, you *have* authority. Stand your ground.

Adopt healthy practices

Consciousness of germs helped people adopt better sanitation, washing their hands more frequently and reducing their contact with waste. As a result, their health began to improve. Follow a similar approach to demons. Do the spiritual equivalent of washing your hands. After working with people afflicted by spirits, ask God to cleanse you and free you from anything that is not of God. That's not a bad prayer to ask regularly, whether you're aware of being around demons or not.

It also would be helpful to start avoiding waste. That doesn't mean avoiding people who need help. That means avoiding things that you know are bad for your spirit and your relationship with God. Ask God to show you what you're in contact with that isn't healthy.

When someone is healed
make sure they fill the empty space

People may wonder about something curious that Jesus said:

> "When the unclean spirit has gone out of a person, it
> wanders through waterless regions looking for a resting
> place, but it finds none. Then it says, 'I will return to my
> house from which I came.' When it comes, it finds it empty,
> swept, and put in order. Then it goes and brings along seven
> other spirits more evil than itself, and they enter and live
> there; and the last state of that person is worse than the first.
> So will it be also with this evil generation." [21]

Sometimes people miss the point of this story and think it
means they shouldn't cast out demons. But if that were the case,
Jesus would never have cast them out himself, and he would not
have told his followers to do the same.

To get to the point of what Jesus meant, think of a bad habit.
You may be able to get rid of it just by will power, for a while.
But if you don't replace the bad habit with something good, you
will eventually be tempted to pick it up again. If you get rid of
a bad habit, you need to replace it with a good one – or even
several good ones. Similarly, if a demon leaves, the person who
was healed needs to fill the space that was previously occupied
with good. One way to do this is to ask God's Spirit to fill you
and to begin doing things Jesus taught that you haven't had the
courage to do yet.

It's not like Hollywood

Every now and then people get their idea of demons from
Hollywood instead of the Bible. Hollywood often portrays
demons and spirits in ways that make them less believable
or that cause people to fear them. They're definitely real, but
you don't need to be afraid of them. Followers of Jesus have
authority over them. Tell them to go.

Checklist

_____ Make a list of vows you have made in the past. If any no longer serve you, replace them with better ideas.

_____ If you encounter a stubborn condition that doesn't respond to medical treatment, tell the spirit causing the condition to go. You can do this even if you're not in the same room.

_____ Ask for the ability to correctly discern hidden things.

_____ If a condition is beyond you, refer the person to someone with more success in that area.

_____ Recognize your authority as a follower of Jesus.

_____ Ask God to cleanse you after encounters with demons.

_____ Fill empty spaces with God's Spirit.

_____ Start great new habits to replace bad ones.

Questions for Discussion

1)   What vows have you made in the past? Do they still serve you?

2)   What do you think about demons? Do you believe they exist?

3)   How much experience have you had casting out demons?

4)   What else in this chapter caught your attention?

Chapter 11

The Effort Is Worth It!

For many of us, the biggest hindrance to praying for others to be healed will be our own fears and inhibitions. Many of us don't want to make a scene, or to appear foolish, or to overpromise, or to be wrong, or to fail. But in many cases, we would have had to endure only a few moments of embarrassment to set someone free from a lifetime of pain. How sad to have such hindrances. May we all become bold in bringing God's kingdom to others!

As we overcome our own internal resistance, we may encounter resistance from others. As far as God is concerned, healing can happen any time, any day of the year. But this view is not always shared by people.

Surprisingly, some people do not want to be healed. They gain benefits like sympathy or income from being ill or they think they are not worthy of being well. Similarly, some people do not want *someone else* to be healed. They somehow benefit and don't want the condition to change. Others object to the *way* that people are healed or to the one who gets the credit.[1] Healing often demonstrates the power of God or Jesus, and some people do not like God being honored and God's power being displayed – they would rather the person stayed sick than have God get the credit for healing the person.

In his lifetime, Jesus was attacked and persecuted for healing others[2] and he taught that we should expect the same when doing similar works.[3] The Bible records that four of his early followers were jailed for healing people.[4]

Healing others may be painful

Much of the Bible describes God's attempts to save us from

the wrong choices we make. The Bible describes how, from the beginning of creation, people have chosen to turn away from God who loves us and to engage in behavior that is harmful. The end result of our harmful choices is death — and the loss of a close relationship with God.

The Bible says that God doesn't want anyone to be separated from God, so Jesus came to earth to create a new way. It says that Jesus was without sin, and when he was tortured to death, he took on himself the punishment that we all deserved. Peter, a contemporary of Jesus, wrote about him:

> He himself bore our sins in his body on the cross, so that, free from sins, we might live for righteousness; by his wounds you have been healed.[5]

The Bible says Jesus accomplished tremendous good on the cross, but the story of that incident shows that healing sometimes comes at agonizing cost. When Jesus died to rescue you and me from the consequences of our harmful choices, Jesus experienced:

* the desertion of friends[6]

* false accusations[7]

* angry crowds[8]

* being mocked[9]

* torture[10]

* the loss of his personal property[11]

* despair[12]

* death[13]

One writer says Jesus endured all those things "for the sake of the joy that was set before him."[14] With his eyes fixed on your and my restoration to the presence of God who loves us, he accepted the suffering. Was it worth it? Yes. Was it painful and difficult to endure? No doubt about it.

Hopefully, none of the things that happened to Jesus at the end of his life will happen to you. But they might. People who heal others are not always respected, and sometimes they are persecuted. The teaching and example of Jesus show that healing (and attempts at healing) should continue in spite of discouragement and opposition.

Ask God for boldness

Peter and John were two of Jesus' initial followers. When they saw a beggar asking for money, Peter told the beggar, "I have no silver or gold, but what I have I give you; in the name of Jesus Christ of Nazareth, stand up and walk." Peter then grabbed the beggar's hand and lifted him up. The Bible says, "immediately his feet and ankles were made strong."[15]

Peter told the amazed witnesses about the power of Jesus – even though speaking about Jesus was forbidden at the time. When Peter and John were brought to court, Peter again testified:

> Let it be known to all of you, and to all the people of Israel, that this man is standing before you in good health by the name of Jesus Christ of Nazareth, whom you crucified, whom God raised from the dead. . . . There is salvation in no one else, for there is no other name under heaven given among mortals by which we must be saved.[16]

The leaders who had opposed Jesus were annoyed by this statement, but they were at a loss what to do since the healed man had been lame for 40 years and he was well known.

It probably was scary for Peter and John to be captured by the very leaders who had crucified Jesus, but when they testified boldly, they saw immediate positive results. Thousands more came to faith.[17] The officials threatened Peter and John and told them not to speak about Jesus any more.

When Peter and John were released from prison, they got together with friends for prayer. They could have asked for safety. They did not. Instead, they asked for boldness to tell even more people about Jesus:

> "Sovereign Lord, . . . grant to your servants to speak your word with all boldness, while you stretch out your hand to heal, and signs and wonders are performed through the name of your holy servant Jesus."[18]

If you need boldness to do the things God has called you to do, you can ask for it like Peter and John did. You can also ask others to pray for you to have enthusiasm and renewed energy when you are discouraged.

Get some practice – the effort is worth it!

Although the cost of praying for healing is sometimes high, the results are worth it. Your prayers can change the course of history.

One of the most helpful things you can do is to get ongoing practice in healing prayer. If you're new to it, find someone who can apprentice you. There are many people in your area who have experience. Talk to them and learn from them. Have them place their hands on you and ask God's Spirit to give you the gift of healing. Then find a good place to practice. (Everywhere.) Form a small group if you haven't yet.

If you're *not* new to this, the same advice applies. It's helpful to learn from the insights of others, to receive prayer from others for an expanded gift of healing, and to practice, no matter what stage we are at. Even experts can improve.

If you are not part of a group that practices healing prayer, there probably is a church near you that does. You could either join one of their midweek home groups or ask to be on their Sunday morning healing team. You'll learn much more quickly if you are around people with experience who can give you the benefit of their observations. Like any aspect of medicine, there is always more to learn. It's often helpful to get training from a church that you haven't visited yet. They may know techniques that are new to you.

In athletics, cross-training is often helpful – that is, training in an area not directly related to your sport. If you haven't seen enough improvement in healing power, start getting some cross-training. Do some things not related to healing that Jesus would approve of. Advance in an "unrelated" area and see what happens – begin tithing, join an evangelism team or a worship team, build a home with Habitat for Humanity for a family that can't afford it, etc. Ask God for some good ideas.

God bless you as you continue to be a healing presence in the world!

Checklist

_____   Take action in spite of your own doubts.

_____   Press on despite opposition.

_____   Ask God for boldness.

_____   Find a mentor.

_____   Have people with experience pray that you receive the gift of healing.

_____   Get in a group that practices praying for healing.

_____   Get some cross-training.

_____   Change the world.

Questions for Discussion

1) Have there been times when you didn't want healing for yourself or others?

2) Have there been times when you didn't want people to pray for healing for yourself or others?

3) What caused you to change? (Or, if you haven't changed yet, what could cause you to change?)

4) What causes you to not reach out to others?

5) Peter and John weren't always bold. But they came to a place in their lives where they were willing to endure imprisonment so others could be healed. Where are you on the boldness scale?

6) Where do you want to be?

7) What have you prayed that has changed the way things were going?

8) What are some areas of cross-training that appeal to you? When will you start trying them out?

9) What else in this chapter caught your attention?

Chapter 12

You Can Transform Nations

You can transform streets, cities and nations with the same techniques that you have learned while for praying for individuals.

If a part of your city is not healthy, you can ask God to heal it, whether it be a piece of land, a group of businesses, an idea held by people, or something else. Tell the condition or the city what to do. Speak to it with the authority of Jesus.

A few reminders:

1) Pray for the nations every chance you get.

2) Move away from people who are scoffing.

3) If you're able, place your hands on a map of the area you are praying for, or walk through the area while you are praying, or find some way to physically touch it, and ask God's power to flow through you.

4) Ask, "God, what would *you* like me to pray about?" Then pray about things you sense in your body, in your mind, in your spirit, and in your heart.

5) If you have doubts while you are praying, don't express them. Instead, pray what the Bible teaches about God's desires for people and the nations.

6) Speak directly to the conditions and tell them what to do.

7) Thank God for any changes you notice.

Checklist

_____ Identify problems you notice in your city, your nation, and the world.

_____ Tell the conditions what to do.

_____ Keep a journal so you remember to thank God for all the answers you see.

Questions for Discussion

1)   What parts of your city are not healthy?

2)   What parts of your nation are not healthy?

3)   What parts of the world are not healthy?

4)   What will you say to these areas to command them to become healthy?

Ideas For Setting Up A Small Group

An easy way to automate praying for others and receiving prayer yourself is to invite a group of friends to discuss this book with you. When you get together, you can read a chapter or part of one, discuss it, and then pray for each other, using the model in chapter three. This way, every time you meet you'll automatically get prayer for your own needs and you'll get practice praying for others. As you compare notes with friends week after week, you'll learn much faster than you would on your own. Here are some tips for your group:

Group size. If you have a group larger than eight, it will be helpful to split into groups of four to eight when you pray for each other. This will give everyone a chance to receive prayer over the course of an hour.

Decide the format for your group

Format. There are lots of ways a discussion group could be organized. One possibility for a one-hour group follows. Let the group members know they need to arrive early or be on time to stick to this tight a schedule.

5 -10 minutes	Talk to people as they arrive.
10 - 20 minutes	Read part of a chapter out loud or have someone summarize it.
10 - 20 minutes	Discuss the questions at the end of the chapter.
20 - 30 minutes	Pray for each other, following the model in chapter three.

Many groups will find that an hour is not enough time. As you begin to open up to each other about problems for which you want prayer, you will probably discover you have plenty to talk about. Sometimes you'll need time to laugh or cry together – or simply to be silent. You may find 1½ or 2 hours to be better.

How much time would you like
to set aside for your group?

Getting started. For many groups, the best way to start may be to invite people to a one-time event to demonstrate what the group will be like. Read the checklist at the end of chapter three and pray for each person in the group, following the steps outlined there. When you're done, find out how many want to get back together the following week to find out what happened. At the second gathering you can pray for each other again and decide how often to meet.

Duration. How many weeks will your group meet together? You could agree to meet once a week for ten weeks or once a month for a year. Each time you could review one chapter and pray for each other. (If you meet monthly instead of weekly, you should plan on your sessions taking a little longer to allow people more time to share experiences.)

Some groups will hesitate to commit to something that long, at least at first. Some might want to meet once a week for a month, just to see how it goes.

Some rules will help your group
be more effective

Rules. Often groups that meet together have rules to help guide the group. Some rules your group will probably want to adopt at its first or second meeting:

1) When it meets, the group will be each participant's top priority. Participants commit to attend a set number of weeks for the sake of themselves and the other members, unless it is

absolutely impossible.

2) Before talking, members in the group can identify things they are about to say as being confidential. At that point, the group can agree to listen or not. If the group agrees to listen, the person's confidence will be kept. People will not discuss the information except within the group.

[An alternative is to say that everything discussed within the group is confidential to the group. Both of these constraints are very difficult for some people to follow.]

3) When it is time for prayer, people in the group are to identify needs of their own. Many times people want to ask for prayer for someone else, which is fine at the end if you have extra time or if people want to stay later. But the group time is set aside to pray for people directly in the group. If each participant identifies a need of his or her own, it will help you learn much faster and it will help you experience what it feels like to receive prayer.

4) No need can be stated more than twice. Some needs are difficult to resolve. Try something else. It may be you've already gotten your request answered and it's just taking time for the answer to get to you. Besides, the group members won't forget your original request. Give them something else to pray about, too.

5) In any given week, much of the time might be focused on one particular person's need. But over the course of the weeks, there will be a balance between time spent for each member of the group. You'll hold to this balance, even if people protest that, compared with other needs, theirs "aren't that important." Each person in the group needs to experience your care.

6) Conversations *about* prayer will never be allowed to take the time for praying itself. You'll learn the most from practicing,

even if continuing to talk feels more comfortable for some members.

7) If you are going to read one or more chapters in advance of your meetings, commit to doing so.

(Requiring advance reading will limit who wants to be in your group and it is not recommended unless you are all very motivated. Some groups will find that it works better to have one person summarize key points for the group. One way to do this would be for the person to use the checklist at the end of each chapter as an outline.)

Notes

Chapter 2

[1.] David Bach tells this story in *The Automatic Millionaire,* New York: Broadway Books, 2004, chapter one.

Chapter 3

[1.] See, for example, Luke 5:15-16. (For help on finding Bible references like "Luke 5:15-16," see the next footnote.) For examples of Jesus praying by himself, see Luke 6:12, 9:18, 9:28, 11:1 and 22:41. For accounts of him healing many people, see Luke 6:18-19 and 9:11 and individual stories throughout the books of Matthew, Mark, Luke and John.

[2.] 1 Thessalonians 5:16-18. This quotation, like many others in this book, is from the Bible.

The Bible is the best-selling book of all time. It is a collection of stories, letters, historical accounts, songs and other forms of literature, written about people interacting with each other and with their creator. Most of the Bible was written between 1,900 and 4,000 years ago in Hebrew, Greek and Aramaic.

Because the Bible is a bestseller and because no one owns the copyright to the original writings, many people and many companies have translated the texts. Current versions are all copyrighted by their translators or publishing companies. As a result, if you go into a bookstore, you might find dozens of Bibles from which to choose.

This book uses quotes from the New Revised Standard Version. Two other popular translations that are easy to read are the New International Version and the New Living Translation.

The Bible is divided into books written by different authors, chapters within the books, and verses within those chapters. Many times I will tell you where a particular quote is found in the Bible. If you want to look it up to see what else is written in the same section, the reference will be written in the format of *Book Chapter: Verse.* For example, the start of this footnote references 1 Thessalonians 5:16-18. *1 Thessalonians* is the name of the book, *5* is the chapter number, and the verses are *16 through 18.*

Go to the index at the start of a Bible to find what page the book 1 Thessalonians starts on. When you find the book, you'll probably see that the chapter starts with a large bold "1." (If it doesn't, scan ahead to find a large bold "2.") That is what chapter numbers look like in the Bible you have. Find the large bold "5" signaling the start of the fifth chapter.

Inside chapter five, you'll find

little numbers indicating the start of verses. If you find the small number sixteen, you'll be at 1 Thessalonians 5:16. Then you'll be able to see how your version translated the passage I quoted.

3. Matthew 13:58.

4. Mark 5:35-43.

5. Mark 9:22-24.

6. Matthew 9:2

7. Luke 18:35-43. See also John 1:38, John 5:6 and Matthew 20:21.

8. See Acts 8:17, 9:17, 19:6. Similarly, the gifts of God's Spirit are sometimes transmitted by touch. See 1 Timothy 4:14 and 2 Timothy 1:6.

9. See, for example, Mark 5:23, 6:5, 8:23-25, and 10 :16, 18; Luke 4:40 and 13:13; and Acts 28:8.

10. See Matthew 8:5-13 and Mark 7:24-30.

11. Jesus told them the execution could be started by anyone who was without sin. One by one, they backed off. See John 7:2-11.

12. John 5:19.

13. Ezekiel had to lie on his left side for 390 days (Ezekiel 4:1-5); Isaiah was told to walk around naked and barefoot for three years (Isaiah 20:1-4); Hosea was commanded to marry a prostitute (Hosea 1:2).

14. Romans 5:7-10.

15. Psalm 139:13.

16. Psalm 139:14.

17. Hebrews 13:5.

18. Matthew 4:23.

19. Hebrews 13:8.

20. Matthew 8:3.

21. Matthew 9:6.

22. Mark 7:34.

23. Mark 1:25 and Mark 9:25. See also Matthew 8:32.

24. Luke 18:42.

25. Luke 13:12.

26. Luke 7:14.

27. Matthew 12:13.

28. Mark 5:41.

29. John 11:43.

30. Mark 4:39.

31. Acts 3:6.

32. Acts 9:34.

33. Acts 9:40.

34. Acts 14:10.

35. Acts 16:18.

36. Matthew 28:19-20.

37. Matthew 22:36-40. See also 1 Corinthians 13:1-3.

38. Matthew 10:8.

39. Mark 8:22-25.

40. Charles G. Finney, *Revival Lectures,* Grand Rapids: Fleming H. Revell, 16.

Chapter 4

1. Psalm 103:1-3.

2. Luke 17:12-19.

3. II Corinthians 1:4.

4. II Kings 20:3.

5. Luke 18:35-43.

Chapter 5

1. Acts 19:11-12.

2. 2 Timothy 4:20.

3. Exodus 5:1-9.

4. This story is in 1 Kings 18:41-45.

5. Daniel 10:12-13.

6. Luke 18:1.

7. Luke 18:2-7.

8. Luke 11:5-10.

9. James 4:1-3.

10. 1 Timothy 2:4.

11. Luke 6:18-19, Revelation 22:2.

12. See Michele Weiner-Davis, *Divorce Busting,* Fireside: New York, 1992. See also Michele Weiner-Davis, *Change Your Life And*

Everyone In It, Fireside: New York, 1995.

[13.] Mark 8:22-26.

[14.] 2 Corinthians 12:9.

[15.] Lewis M. Andrews, PhD, *To Thine Own Self Be True: The Relationship Between Spiritual Values and Emotional Health.* New York: Doubleday, 1987.

[16.] John 5:5-9.

[17.] Luke 8:43-48.

[18.] Acts 9:36-41 and Acts 20:9-12.

[19.] Luke 18:1.

Chapter 6

[1.] Luke 10:29-37.

[2.] Bernie Siegel, *Love, Medicine and Miracles: Lessons Learned about Self-Healing from a Surgeon's Experience with Exceptional Patients.* New York: Harper Paperbacks, 1986.

[3.] A classic text discussing this phenomenon is *Psycho-cybernetics: A New Way To Get More Living Out Of Life* by Maxwell Maltz. Wilshire Book Company: Hollywood, 1960.

[4.] This story from 1 Kings 18:41-46 was discussed in chapter five.

[5.] 2 Kings 5:13.

[6.] 2 Kings 5:14.

[7.] I am not suggesting you take the claims of people without checking their references and track record. You wouldn't want to take medicine without reading the label and knowing the reputation of the doctor and the dispensing pharmacy. The same goes for people offering to treat you.

[8.] Steve Sjogren related his story at the 2003 Robert H. Schuller Institute for Successful Church Leadership. You can read about his experience

in Steve's book, *The Day I Died: An Unforgettable Story of Life After Death.* Ventura: Regal, 2006.

Chapter 7

[1.] Other passages you can look at referring to the correspondence between wrong action and suffering and between right action and healing include:

Exodus 15:26
Deuteronomy 28:15, 27
2 Samuel 12:15
Psalm 38:3
Psalm 107:17-20
Proverbs 3:7-8
Proverbs 4:20-22
Proverbs 29:1
Isaiah 6:10 (quoted in Matthew 13:15, John 12:40, and Acts 28:27)
Isaiah 47:10-11
Jeremiah 8:14
Jeremiah 30:15
Lamentations 2:14
Hosea 6:11b-7:2a
Micah 3:11-12
Amos 4:6-13
Malachi 4:2
Acts 4:34-5:13
1 Corinthians 11:30
Hebrews 12:13

[2.] James 5:16.

[3.] An excellent book that discusses the connection between behavior and health is Lewis Andrews' *To Thine Own Self Be True: The Relationship Between Spiritual Values and Emotional Health.* It's worth a look if other people would describe you as critical, resentful, or the like.

[4.] Exodus 15:26.

[5.] See the references in footnote one for this chapter.

6. You know this by experience. It is a major theme of the Bible, beginning with the first story of human activity, in Genesis 3:11-13.

7. Psalm 73:3-13.

8. Job 1:8-21.

9. John 9:2-3.

10. Anthony Robbins, *Awaken the Giant Within: How to take immediate control of your mental, emotional, physical and financial destiny.* New York: Summit Books, 1991, 128.

11. Ibid., 132.

12. Ibid., 131, 133. For more ideas related to these five steps, see chapter six, "How to Change Anything in Your Life: The Science of Neuro-Associative Conditioning™," in *Awaken the Giant Within,* pp. 128-155. It would be worth it to study this chapter. You can also get specific help from Michele Weiner-Davis' book *Change Your Life and Everyone In It.*

13. Luke 18:1-5.

Chapter 8

1. Revelation 21:1-5.

2. This adaptation of Psalm 23 is based on the King James Version.

Chapter 9

1. See Matthew 19:26, Luke 1:37, and Luke 18:27.

2. See, for example, Matthew 13:54-58.

3. See John 15:4-5.

4. James 4:2. See also Matthew 7:7-11.

5. In a few cases the phrase "in God's name" is used as an oath. See Nehemiah 13:25 and 1 Samuel 20:42 as examples. Sometimes the phrase is used to convey the idea of giving credit. Thus when Esther told a king about a plot, she did so "in the name of Mordecai." In other words, she gave credit to Mordecai, her source for the information. Much of the time, however, the phrase means doing something in the place of another, as that person's representative or as if you were that person. For examples of this kind of usage see Deuteronomy 18:5-7, Jeremiah 11:21, Matthew 24:5 and John 14:26. This is the sense that best fits the passage from John.

6. People who are disobedient can be still be effective if they are gifted or have other compensating factors. But they would be even more effective if they were obedient. That's why it's helpful to know what God wants. If you've never read the Bible, find the book of Matthew and start there. Matthew and the three books after it have descriptions of Jesus healing people.

7. 1 Corinthians 12:8-11.

8. 1 Corinthians 12:31.

9. You can see examples at http://www.MarkDahle.com

10. *Outliers: The Story of Success,* Malcolm Gladwell. New York: Little Brown and Company, 2008, chapter two.

11. In Mark 9:29, Jesus says prayer is required to cast out some kinds of demons. The footnote to this verse in most Bibles adds that many ancient versions also list fasting as something Jesus said was required.

12. See Matthew 4:2 and Luke 5:33-35 for his teaching on this. See Acts 13:2-3 and Acts 14:23 for examples of times when they followed through.

13. Luke 18:12.

14. Zechariah 7:5.
15. Matthew 6:16-18.
16. Mark 6:5-6.
17. Mark 11:24.
18. Maxwell Maltz, *Psycho-cybernetics: A New Way To Get More Living Out Of Life.* Wilshire Book Company: Hollywood, 1960, 47-49.
19. See Matthew 17:18-20 and Matthew 21:19-22. Other examples from Matthew: 8:8-10, 8:24-26, 9:20-22, 9:27-29, 14:22-31, 15:22-28, 23:23.
20. Mark 9:24.
21. John Kilpatrick, *Feast of Fire.* Brownsville Assembly of God: Pensacola, 1995, 51.
22. Ibid, 52.
23. James 1:6-8.

Chapter 10

1. Some habits are stubborn and require significant effort to change. But you can change anything. For stubborn cases, see the excellent book *Change Anything: The New Science of Personal Success,* by Kerry Patterson, Joseph Grenny, David Maxfield, Ron McMillan, and Al Switzler. Business Plus: New York, 2011.
2. Acts 23:8.
3. See, for example, Matthew 4:24, Matthew 8:16, Matthew 8:28-34, and Matthew 15:21-28. For the links to illness, see footnotes 8 through 11.
4. See footnote 2.
5. Mark 6:7,13, Mark 3:14-15, Mark 16:17, Luke 9:1.
6. Mark 6:13, Acts 5:16, Acts 8:7, Acts 19:12.
7. Matthew 8:29, Mark 3:11, Luke 4:41.
8. Mark 1:26, Mark 9:26, Acts 8:7.

9. Matthew 9:32-33.
10. Luke 13:11-13.
11. Matthew 17:14-18.
12. Mark 5:1-20.
13. Mark 5:1-20.
14. Mark 5:1-20.
15. Luke 10:17.
16. Mark 9:29
17. For one example, see Acts 3:1-3.
18. For one example, see Matthew 15:1-9.
19. Mark 9:38, Matthew 7:22-23
20. Acts 19:13-17
21. Matthew 12:43-45

Chapter 11

1. See, for instance, Mark 2:7, 3:2-6, 3:21-22; 5:15-17, 6:2-3; 6:54-56.
2. Matthew 12:22-24.
3. Matthew 10:18-22.
4. For the story about Peter and John see Acts 4:1-22. About Peter, see Acts 5:14-18. About Paul and Silas, Acts 16:18-23.
5. 1 Peter 2:24.
6. Matthew 26:56 and 74.
7. Matthew 26:59-60.
8. Matthew 27:22.
9. Matthew 27:28-29.
10. Matthew 27:29-30.
11. Matthew 27:35.
12. Matthew 27:46.
13. Matthew 27:50.
14. Hebrews 12:2.
15. Acts 3:7.
16. Acts 4:10-12.
17. Acts 4:4. A few days before this incident, the number of disciples stood at 3,000; afterwards it was 5,000.
18. Acts 4:24-30.

63150089R00088

Made in the USA
Lexington, KY
28 April 2017